MIDRASH AND THEORY

Rethinking Theory

GENERAL EDITOR

Gary Saul Morson

CONSULTING EDITORS

Robert Alter
Frederick Crews
John M. Ellis
Caryl Emerson

Midrash and Theory

Ancient Jewish Exegesis and Contemporary Literary Studies

David Stern

Northwestern University Press
Evanston, Illinois

Northwestern University Press
Evanston, Illinois 60208-4210

Published 1996

Printed in the United States of America
First paperback printing 1997
ISBN 0-8101-1574-3

Library of Congress Cataloging-in-Publication Data

Stern, David, 1949–
Midrash and theory : ancient Jewish exegesis and contemporary literary studies/David Stern.
p. cm.—(Rethinking theory)
Includes bibliographical references and index.
ISBN 0-8101-1574-3 (alk. paper)
1. Midrash—History and criticism. 2. Midrash—History and criticism—Theory, etc. 3. Parables in rabbinical literature. 4. God (Judaism). I. Title. II. Series.
BM514.S745 1996
296.1'406'01—dc20 96-1076
CIP

The paper used in this publication meets the minimum requirements of the American National Standard for Information Sciences—Permanence of Paper for Printed Library Materials, ANSI Z39.48-1984.

Contents

Acknowledgments vii

Introduction: The Midrash-Theory Connection 1

Chapter 1 Midrash and Hermeneutics: Polysemy vs. Indeterminacy 15

Chapter 2 Forms of Midrash I: Parables of Interpretation 39

Chapter 3 Forms of Midrash II: Homily and the Language of Exegesis 55

Chapter 4 Midrash and Theology: The Character(s) of God 73

Notes 95

Index 117

For Kathryn,
With much love

Acknowledgments

Every book has its own history. This book's history happens to mirror its subject, the linkage forged between midrash and literary theory in the contemporary American university. The chapters in this book all began their lives as presentations or papers presented at various interdisciplinary university seminars: the Columbia University Seminar on Literary Theory, the Center for Literary Studies at the Hebrew University, the Whitney Humanities Center at Yale University, the Jewish Studies Workshop at the University of Chicago, and the Humanities Center at the University of California at Irvine. Each of these seminars was itself an example of the kind of intellectual dialogue that created the midrash-theory linkage, and I wish to thank the organizers and chairpersons of the seminars for giving me the initial incentive to write these essays as well as the participants for their comments and reactions.

The work of revising and turning these essays into this book was done largely during my tenure as a fellow of the Program in Alternative Thinking at Tel Aviv University during the academic year of 1994–95. I wish to thank both my host, Professor Meir Sternberg, the director of the program, and the Porter Institute at Tel Aviv University and its director, Professor Ziva Ben-Porat, for providing me with so congenial a work environment. My close friend and colleague Alan Mintz read the entire revised manuscript with his usual intelligence and sensitivity. Geoffrey Hartman kindly read and commented upon the introductory essay. Finally, I owe a special debt of gratitude to Gary Saul Morson, the editor of the distinguished series in which this book appears; to Peter Hayes, the chair of the editorial board of Northwestern University Press, for encouraging me to put this book together; and to Nick Weir-Williams, the director of the Press, for his patience in making that possible. Ellen Feldman has copyedited the manuscript with wonderful thoughtfulness, and with an eye for consistency and detail that would have been the envy of any ancient midrashist.

Of an entirely different order is my debt of gratitude to Kathryn Hellerstein, my partner in yidrash, to whom this book is dedicated with much love and affection.

Chapters 1–4 originally appeared in somewhat different form as independent essays and appear here by permission:

Chapter 1, "Midrash and Hermeneutics: Polysemy vs. Indeterminacy," was first published in *Critical Inquiry* 15 (Autumn 1988) as "Midrash and Indeterminacy."

Chapter 2, "Forms of Midrash I: Parables of Interpretation," was first published as "The Rabbinic Parable and the Narrative of Interpretation," in *The Midrashic Imagination: Jewish Exegesis, Thought, and History,* edited by Michael Fishbane (Albany, 1993). Copyright © 1993 by the State University of New York Press. By permission of the State University of New York Press.

Chapter 3, "Forms of Midrash II: Homily and the Language of Exegesis," was first published as "Midrash and the Language of Exegesis," in *Midrash and Literature,* edited by Geoffrey Hartman and Sanford Budick (New Haven, Conn., 1986). Copyright © 1986 by Yale University Press. By permission of Yale University Press.

Chapter 4, "Midrash and Theology: The Character(s) of God," was first published in *Prooftexts* 12 (1992) as "*Imitatio Hominis:* Anthropomorphism and the Character(s) of God in Rabbinic Literature." By permission of The Johns Hopkins University Press.

For permission to reprint these essays in revised form, I wish to thank the above publishers.

Introduction

The Midrash-Theory Connection

This is a book about reading midrash, the literature of classical Jewish Scriptural interpretation, and about the challenges that this act of reading involves. As such, this book is about an *experience* as much as a subject, and about how that experience has changed in the recent past.

The major impetus for this change has come from the encounter of midrash scholarship with contemporary literary studies—structuralism, semiotics, deconstruction, cultural studies, indeed virtually all the modes of postmodernism as they have come into fashion and gone out of it. Under the impact of theory, midrash has gone through a veritable sea change. The focus of the field, its methods, its conceptual premises, have all experienced a fundamental, radical transformation. And during the same period, midrash has gained a currency within the larger intellectual world that it never possessed before, particularly within literary circles. For a short time, midrash has even been a "hot" topic.

How lasting and deep the impact of midrash has been on literary theory remains an open question. At the least, midrash has provided a vantage point on literary interpretation from which its modern phase can be seen to be but the very tip of the iceberg. If only in this way, the inclusion of midrash has enlarged the canon of theoretical criticism, and its enlargment may be still greater yet. By including midrash within its compass, criticism "would exercise its power to revalue an alienated practice," as Geoffrey Hartman, the most impassioned advocate for midrash in wider literary circles, has argued. Criticism would thus "restitute" itself and, by increasing our awareness of the possibilities of creative exegesis, immeasurably enrich our textual imaginations.[1]

My purpose here, however, is to ask not what midrash can do for literary criticism but what theory has done to midrash. For one thing, it has raised a series of questions that, while not entirely new or unanticipated, have now become explicit topics of debate. Foremost among these is the question of the contemporary significance of midrash—its cultural relevance, as it were—and the connection between that cultural relevance and what scholars like to call the meaning of midrash "in its own terms," that is, within its original historical and literary context. Where do these two meet? How does one cast the meaning of midrash in the contemporary terms of, say, literary theory without distorting its integrity? Or, what is really at issue, without distorting it *too* much? To what extent is a historicist approach to midrash, as a subject of primarily antiquarian interest, truly opposed to a more literary, humanistic, and theoretical appreciation of its significance? Or, to put the same question differently, how are we to secularize our understanding of this inherently religious literature, as we must, without profaning it?

These questions are neither unique nor specific to midrash. They concern the entire project of retrieving Jewish tradition in our times. But for a number of reasons—a surge of interest in midrash as a mode of popular spirituality within the wider Jewish community, the discovery of midrash as a literary tradition by contemporary Jewish writers—these questions have now emerged most urgently in relation to the way midrash has come to be studied in the last decade or two. This book is essentially a response to such questions. What it offers, though, is not so much a definitive answer or resolution as a stance—an attempt to forge what is, I hope, an approach that is both responsible and responsive, true to the literary integrity of classical Jewish literature and yet open to our desire for this literature to mean something to us. Precisely in order to make midrash speak to us in contemporary language, I have sought in this book to develop a way of talking about midrash that uses theory as a bridge, as a means of spanning the distance between the classical sources and ourselves.

This book was conceived during the same period as the midrash-theory connection developed, and the story of that connection is, in large part, the history behind its writing. The first thing to say about this story is that it was a particularly American tale, and American in a number of ways. Not only were most of the figures involved in it Americans, and not only did much of it transpire in America (the major exception being a yearlong seminar held at Hebrew University in Jerusalem in 1983–84, which culminated in the widely read collection of essays *Midrash and Literature*),[2] but even the very linkage between midrash and theory was shaped by the environment of the American university in the late 1970s and early 1980s. In fact, it is virtually impossible to imagine the midrash-theory connection having been created at any other time and outside that specific institutional context, that is, precisely when a tidal wave of change first swept over the university's until-then impregnable walls. This wave of change included the breakdown of the strict boundaries that previously had separated distinct academic disciplines and departments; the shifting of attention away from the centers of "high" culture—male, white, classical, Christian—toward the various "others"—feminist, ethnic, "low," popular—that formerly inhabited only the peripheries and margins of academic study; and, perhaps most prominently, the emergence of critical theory, in its manifold versions, as a kind of new academic lingua franca, a specialized, sometimes quasi-esoteric discourse of self-reflection and self-examination concerned with its own workings and with the situation of criticism itself.

Under the new dominion of theory, many separate fields—anthropology, literature, linguistics, music, the history of science—previously unrelated and hardly known to each other suddenly found themselves thrown together and engaged in genuine dialogue, often in the service of creating a kind of new critical metadiscourse. And among all of these shifting realignments, none, perhaps, was more surprising than the midrash-theory linkage.

The initial impetus for this linkage came primarily from literary theory. For some time, in fact, literary studies in America had been in the process of what one critic has called its "dehellenization," repudiating both the formalism of the New Critics and the genteel (and Gentile) civility of much previous academic literary study.[3] As many of its old verities came under attack, the literary profession reopened the question perhaps most basic to its discipline: What is literature? This question could take several forms: Wherein lies the uniqueness of the work of literary art? How can one define literature as opposed to other types of discourse? What is the difference between literature and commentary or criticism? But whatever form it took, the effect of the question was to shatter the overly narrow definition of literature that previously had governed literary study in the academy. Further, by breaking the stranglehold of "literature" as a narrow category that included only a few select, special, canonical texts, literary study itself could now be extended to all sorts of writing that heretofore had not fallen under the conventional rubric. Foremost among these were literary theory and criticism themselves, which could now escape their secondary status and aspire to be read as forms of writing no less creative and original than what generally passed under the name of "literature."

This was the institutional and intellectual context in which the midrash-theory connection was forged. Essentially, two types of scholars were involved in making the connection: on the one side were a few younger students and scholars in Jewish studies, many of whom (myself included) had entered the field with academic backgrounds in either English or comparative literature; on the other were several critics and theorists from the general literary world (many though not all of them Jewish), a number of whom were very distinguished figures, thus lending a kind of immediate prestige to the new interest in midrash that it otherwise never would have possessed. For all their differences, both groups of scholars found themselves fascinated by precisely the same wayward, antic features of midrashic interpretation that had often been considered scandalous in the past. The typical midrashic predilection for multiple interpretations rather than for a single truth behind the text; its irresistible desire to tease out the nuances of Scripture rather than use interpretation to close them off; and, most of all, the way midrashic discourse mixes text and commentary, violating the boundaries between them and intentionally blurring their differences, flourishing precisely in the grayish no-man's-land between exegesis and literature—all these features that once had seemed (since the time of Maimonides at least) to be the most problematic and irrational aspects of midrash now became its most intriguing, fascinating qualities.

Within Jewish studies, the sudden flurry of interest in midrash was almost unprecedented. For the first time in memory, the academy seemed to be authentically excited about something Jewish—other than the Hebrew Bible, of course, which long ago had been appropriated by Christian scholars, even in its most recent avatar as "Bible as literature." Although the midrash-theory connection followed closely on the latter's heel—and was to a certain extent enabled and facilitated by its academic success—the literary approach to midrash was also inherently different from the Bible-as-literature movement (in all its varieties). Essentially, the literary approach to the Bible was an effort to use the concept of "literature" as a way of "saving" the Bible, of reconstituting the wholeness of the biblical text, of recapturing a textual integrity and coherence that had been shattered by modern critical and historical study of the Bible. For at least some of its practitioners, the literary approach also provided a means for recuperating the humanistic significance of the Bible as a cultural artifact. By placing the Bible under the purview of "literature," it became possible to argue for its continuing cultural authority as a secular document without adopting a purely historicizing, inevitably distancing and estranging, stance toward its meaning.[4] In contrast, the midrash-theory connection was less an attempt to "save" midrash than it was an effort to find a genealogy, a precursor, for theory itself. As an interdisciplinary linkage, the connection presumed that midrash was in some sense an embryonic form of theory, a mode of interpretation that must be understood alongside other modes of interpretive method and practice. It was thus less an attempt to use "literature" to recuperate the meaning of midrash as an effort to show that midrash, too, was literature. Indeed, the implied argument was that learning to read midrash as a mode of discourse might even enhance our notion of what literature is, or could be. Thus, the transgressive character of midrash—the nonchalance with which it consistently violates the boundaries between text and commentary—was certainly one source of the powerful fascination that midrash commanded among post-structuralist theorists. Moreover, the interdisciplinary linkage between midrash and theory could itself claim some of that same transgressiveness. This quality of the slightly forbidden was only enhanced by the Gothic, Byzantine complexity of midrashic discourse, its unassimilated foreignness, which may have seemed to represent a kind of *echt* Judaism that heretofore had scarcely been tolerated within the proper and Protestant walls of the American university, let alone allowed full admission into its corridors.

To be certain, the interdisciplinary nature of the linkage between midrash and literary theory soon led to tension. Students of midrash, despite their commitment to theory, were interested mainly in using it as an instrument for opening up midrash, as a tool for clarifying and delineating their often baffling yet beguiling subject. Early on, however, they found that midrashic literature resisted many of the categories and phenomena that post-structuralist theory had initially seemed to open up for them. For example, the notion of indeterminacy was not as helpful as many had first supposed it would be for understanding midrashic polysemy, a subject I discuss at length in chapter 1. In this way, the act of studying midrash from the perspective of theory itself became a process of distancing, even of disillusionment with theory's imperializing claim that it could comprehend and subsume all writing.

Still, the vantage point that theory offered from which to view midrash, along with its value as a lexicon of critical terminology and conceptual categories, was revolutionary. An entirely new vision of the field was revealed. In a short time articles and books appeared using narratology, rhetorical criticism, and semiotics to analyze midrashic texts; other studies sought to apply such critical notions as intertextuality, Bakhtinian dialogics, and methodologies drawn more eclectically from both philosophical and theological hermeneutics, from thinkers like Gadamer and Ricoeur, to the task of "theorizing" midrash.[5] The contributions of these studies, both large and small, were substantive, even though the question still remained as to the degree to which midrash was, in fact, susceptible to theorizing—that is, to being systematically analyzed and described within any single conceptual framework, no matter how flexible or eclectic. In some cases, the very recalcitrance and obscurity of the midrashic texts themselves, as well as their generic status as documents, called into doubt the very conclusions such "theories" of midrash wished to draw.[6]

On the other side of the linkage, literary critics and theoreticians also encountered resistance to the project. For one thing, they had their own agenda in studying midrash. Especially for critics whose approaches were aligned more closely with deconstruction, part of that agenda was a desire to create an alternative interpretive tradition, a way to combat the logocentrism that, so it was argued, had ruled literary discourse in the West, or, as it was sometimes called, the Greco-Christian tradition.[7] As it was constructed, this alternative nonlogocentric tradition was said to begin with midrash (or with the Hebrew Bible as a kind of proto-midrashic text) and to end with deconstruction.[8]

It became clear early on that there were difficulties with this construction. For one thing, the opposition between midrash and logocentric interpretation, which was largely identified with the allegorical tradition, was essentially a new recasting of the age-old battle between Hebraism and Hellenism. Yet the latter, one of the commomplaces of Western cultural history, presents special difficulties when it is applied to the history of Judaism and its culture. Foremost among these is the fact that classical Judaism, the Judaism of the Rabbis who created midrash, was itself (as scholars over the last century have definitively established) a fusion that derived from the confrontation between native Israelite tradition and Hellenism, the culture of ancient Greece and Rome.[9] That is to say, Rabbinic Judaism is already a mixture, a mingling of Israelite, or biblical, and Greco-Roman elements. And so is its foremost literary creation, midrash. Far from being inherently opposed to allegory, midrash is at times—though not always and certainly not exclusively—deeply allegorical in its modes of interpretation.

Further, the connection between midrash and deconstruction—the alpha and omega, as it were, of this nonlogocentric tradition of interpretation—presumed a historical bond that was impossible to trace, let alone prove. The link became even more tenuous when many of the presumed similarities between midrash and post-structuralism—like those between modern textual indeterminacy and midrashic polysemy—were found to be, on closer examination, not as similar as initially thought.

Inevitably, the emotional and intellectual investments that both types of new readers of midrash brought to their studies created conflicts and tensions. In the very course of interdisciplinary dialogue, as midrash specialists pointed out the flaws in some of the theorists' presuppositions, they (the specialists) suddenly found themselves cast into the role of jealous guardians of the temple, while the theorists felt they were being portrayed as trespassers in the holy precinct. On the other hand, the theorists sought to depict themselves as the authentic heirs of the midrashic tradition; this, after all, was the essence of their claim to the continuity between the midrashic tradition and the post-structuralist stance. From this perspective, the midrash specialists were revealed to be closet positivists, old-fashioned philologists incapable of acknowledging the truly radical originality of midrash and concerned only with defending their scholarly turf. The specialists responded to this accusation, in turn, by claiming that, far from trying to prevent access to their subject, they were simply trying to do justice to its real uniqueness, which was inextricably tied to its difficult, often philologically problematic, complexity.[10]

A good part of this conflict may have been an inevitable by-product of interdisciplinary study in the contemporary university setting. Indeed, the case of midrash and literature was an almost perfect exemplification of the strengths and weaknesses of interdisciplinarity. It showed the kinds of fresh insights that "outsiders," nonspecialists, are able to bring to a field, and the flaws that such radical and original insights may have precisely because their authors are not specialists. To be sure, such difficulties can occur in any interdisciplinary project, but they are most likely to arise in fields like midrash that, because of their unique philological characteristics, require some type of specialized training in order to be able to master their texts (although the tyranny and monomania of specialization is also the most compelling reason why such fields can benefit greatly from the distanced view that only a nonspecialist can provide).

Nonetheless, the conflict that developed, even if inevitable, was truly unfortunate, because it obscured the extent to which both sides shared an appreciation of midrash as a truly rich and complex form of literature to be read in its own right, not merely as a commentary on the Bible or as an adjunct to some other field of inquiry. It also obscured the degree to which both types of new readings of midrash represented a decisive break with the way midrash had been studied in the academy since the establishment of Die Wissenschaft des Judentums, the ancestor of modern Jewish studies, in the early nineteenth century. Indeed, in the eyes of more traditional scholars in Rabbinics, both camps—the so-called "literary midrash specialists" and the "theorists interested in midrash"—were equally suspect, similarly dismissed as jargon-mongerers whose writings mystified their subjects more than they made substantive—"scientific"—contributions to our knowledge of midrash. For these scholars, the literary approach in any of its varieties seemed more like postmodern homiletics than real scholarship, that is, the type of scholarship that had "rescued" midrash from the dustbin of religious obscurantism when, with the collapse of traditional Jewish life and the onset of modernity, much of classical Jewish literature had been threatened by oblivion.

The truth is that the new literary approach to midrash was not the beginning of the modern study of midrash. Nor had midrash been neglected or suppressed before its discovery by the literary scholars and critics (as, say, Jewish mystical literature is often said to have been suppressed by the apologetic rationalism of Jewish scholarship before its great recovery earlier in this century). In fact, the recovery and rehabilitation of midrash (along with its generic corollary, aggadah, that is, Rabbinic legend or lore) had been one of Wissenschaft's major projects. Perhaps the single greatest work to be produced by the entire school of Wissenschaft was Leopold Zunz's *Die gottesdienstlichen Vortraege der Juden historisch entwickelt*, a work that raised the "Science of Judaism" to the rank of a scholarly discipline and remains to this day the most complete literary history of midrashic literature.[11] Following Zunz, one can trace a line of important scholars of midrash in both America and Israel who laid the groundwork for recognition of its literariness. Among these, special mention should be made of three individuals: Isaac (Yitzhak) Heinemann and Max Kadushin, who independently made the first (and somewhat similar) efforts at presenting "theories" of midrash that departed radically from traditional hermeneutical approaches; and Joseph Heinemann, who, although not a theoretician or trained critic, brought an acute literary sensitivity to the study of midrash.[12] In the early 1970s, Heinemann was appointed to a professorship in midrash in the department of Hebrew literature at Hebrew University in Jerusalem. This was perhaps the ultimate sign that midrash had "arrived" as a fully recognized subject within the Jewish literary curriculum.

Even so, the midrash-theory connnection was different. Despite all the recognition that its literary features had received, midrash was still largely studied in the university within departments of Rabbinic literature, as a province of Talmudic literature, and with an emphasis on law over lore.[13] And even when it was studied in these ways, midrash, like Talmud, was treated primarily as a foundational document of Judaism, important either for its religious value and meaning or as an ancient source to be mined for historical and philological information about early Judaism and Christianity. Where it was recognized for its exegetical interest, this was almost exclusively for the purposes of comparative exegesis, the tracing of the history of a given interpretation through different historical periods and religious traditions. Important as such study was, it ignored almost entirely the form of midrash, concentrating instead on its substance, the content of exegesis. On the other hand, when more literary-minded scholars did try to study midrash as "literature," they tended to do so at the expense of its exegetical dimension, which was viewed as being inimical in some way to its so-called literary features.[14]

In contrast, the new literary study of midrash aimed to demonstrate that midrash *was* a literature of interpretation, that its literary character was intrinsically bound up with its exegetical dimension. More than that, it sought to show how midrash could be viewed as the embodiment of an authentic, native Jewish creativity, which, it was now understood, was in no way inimical to the exegetical tradition within Judaism; to the contrary, midrash became the paradigm for exegesis as a creative religious and imaginative act. This recognition was, arguably, the single most important contribution of the midrash-theory connection. But what was most remarkable about this new perception—the ability to see the process of interpretation not only as the method but also as the very essence of the literary nature of midrash—is that it was made possible only through exposure to modernist writers and critics like Franz Kafka, Jorge Luis Borges, Walter Benjamin, and Roland Barthes, whose writings similarly compound text and exegesis. If we had not first learned how to read these modernists, we would never have known how to read midrash. They provided the lens through which we were first able to recognize the singular literary-exegetical features that are visible in midrash as well as in modernist texts.

The moment of interdisciplinary excitement I have sketched out here has now largely passed. With the demise of deconstruction, literary theorists—with a few notable exceptions, like Geoffrey Hartman, whose work and personal example have exerted a major influence upon the field[15]—seem to have lost interest in midrash and in other aspects of classical Judaism and its literature. Harold Bloom has turned his attention from Kabbalah and its relation to criticism to a wholesale Gnostic rejection of all "normative" Judaism (which suggests how little Bloom ever understood about Kabbalah's presence within "normative" Judaism). More sadly, Jewish studies, no longer understood as the repressed or suppressed "other" of Western culture, is now perceived as part of the hegemonic cultural imperialism that has suppressed and continues to suppress all the minority voices within that culture, the supposedly authentic voices of multiculturalism and pluralism.

Yet whatever its fate in the larger literary theoretical world, the midrash-theory connection has had a lasting impact on the study of midrash. Indeed, now that the buzz and flurry of the initial excitement has passed, the time has arrived to reap the fruits of the original linkage and to begin the real work of reading midrash theoretically, as literary discourse—that is, to use the theoretical sophistication appropriated from literary studies to describe midrash's literary forms in their specificity and full complexity; to use the language of midrash as the base from which to discuss its hermeneutics in the light of the history of interpretation; and, perhaps most importantly, to employ our growing knowledge of the social, religiopolitical, and gender constructions of literature in order to analyze the singular forms of Rabbinic writing. The chapters in this book seek to offer modest examples of what such a work of reading might entail, and of the different kinds of theoretical and literary challenges that it inevitably faces.

The full impact of the midrash-theory connection has not been limited to the field of midrash scholarship alone. Its repercussions have spread not only into such cognate areas as Talmud, Kabbalah, and medieval Hebrew literature, but also into the field of Jewish studies as a whole, for which midrash has, in effect, functioned as a kind of avant-garde, an advance force through which Jewish studies as a discipline has engaged the frontiers of the humanities within the American university. Indeed, the impact of the interdisciplinary linkage upon Jewish studies has been so great that it is worth reflecting for a moment upon its significance and especially why its ripplelike effects have been so extensive.

I would suggest that a good part of the reason for this has to do with the identity politics of Jewish studies, namely, the ways in which the modern academic and critical study of Judaism, since its inception in Wissenschaft, has participated in shaping Jewish selfhood in the modern world. As many historians have noted, modern Jewish scholarship has always served diverse ideological purposes. In its earlier periods alone, these purposes ranged from Moritz Steinschneider's somewhat overworked formulation that the duty of the historian is to give "the remains of Judaism a decent burial," to functioning as a tool of emancipation and assimilation into Western culture, or serving as an instrument for the reform and revivification of Judaism.[16]

Somewhat more intimately, the study of the past has also worked as "a personal exercise in group genealogy," as the historian David Myers has written.[17] Since the Enlightenment, Jewish scholars have explored their Jewishness through intellectual immersion in the foundational texts of the past, from the Bible through the great medieval classics, even though they have ceased to believe in those texts the way that the texts claim their readers must. That is to say, since the beginning of the modern period, the critical study of Jewish texts has been a primary mode of establishing Jewishness as a *secular* identity. This was certainly the case with the modern study of midrash from Zunz's time onward.

It was precisely here, however, that the new literary study of midrash differed not only from more traditional midrash scholarship but also from the mainstream of Jewish studies. "The primary intellectual encounter between Judaism and modern culture has been precisely in a mutual preoccupation with the historicity of things," Yosef Hayim Yerushalmi has written in his eloquent study of Jewish history and memory, *Zakhor*.[18] Most modern Jewish scholarship, indeed most intellectual concern with things Jewish, has been dominated by the study of history, with the recovery and reconstruction of the Jewish past in its fullness. Yet precisely because of this historicist orientation, as Yerushalmi has lamented, the modern Jewish historian (read scholar) cannot escape "the ironic awareness that the very mode" in which he or she delves into the past "represents a decisive break with that past."[19] This is the modern Jewish scholar's malaise. If history, in Yerushalmi's apt formulation, has been "the faith of fallen Jews,"[20] it has been a faith that has not been able to recreate the wholeness of our forebears' belief, nor has it been able to heal the wounds that modernity has inflicted upon the collective Jewish memory, indeed upon collective Jewish existence.

To some extent, the midrash-theory connection sought to overcome this melancholy awareness of the failure of historicism. Not exactly theological in its tenor but not without some implicit theological aspirations, not entirely oblivious to historical considerations but not at all antiquarian in its orientation, the midrash-theory connection hoped to discover in midrash a form of Jewish creativity that could be transmissable, reclaimable, in a way that purely historicist knowledge about the Jewish past could never be. Undoubtedly, part of this desire to find in literature a form of creativity that could somehow defeat history and offer a kind of surrogate for the wholeness, the spiritual redemption, once offered by religion was a vestige of late Romanticism and on that count perhaps doomed to frustration from the beginning. Nor am I suggesting that it was ever possible for midrash scholarship—whether of the new literary or the more traditional philological variety—to escape the dilemmas of historicism (any more than the literary approach to the Bible succeeded in avoiding a confrontation with more historicist readings of the biblical text). Nonetheless, the persistence of the desire to overcome the knowledge of a decisive break with the past—a break in whose shadow we live—and to find in midrash a kind of hermeneutical metanarrative that would transcend the ironic awareness of history is powerful testimony to the dissatisfaction with pure historicism as a mode of Jewish intellectual conduct.[21] The genuine vitality that characterized the midrash-theory connection, the sheer intellectual excitement of the encounter, attests to the possibility of finding within Jewish tradition a mode of creativity that is more than just historical knowledge, that is still able to evoke real excitement among contemporary Jews.

We must not, of course, exaggerate the impact of the midrash-theory connection. Even if it is true that the university is the primary site in the world today for original and creative thinking on questions of Jewishness (be they theological or demographic in orientation), we would do well to remember how restricted and limited the academic world can be. As one writer has said recently about the possibility of midrash to serve as a source for contemporary religious discourse, "Outside the world of the academy, in the lives of Jews who know very little about this literature, midrash is a strange animal. There is in these texts a whole dimension of difficulty."[22] This includes not only the inability to accept the beliefs that undergird midrash—its assumptions about the nature of Torah, for example, as a divinely authored text—and its religious messages, which may or may not conform to our ideas of Jewish faith (if we identify as Jews, and even less obviously if we do not). Even more importantly, the reading of midrash, because of the obscure, sometimes arcane nature of its texts, inevitably disappoints and frustrates the expectations of *personal* meaningfulness that a reader who is not an academic brings to these texts, the hunger to have these texts connect *immediately* to one's identity (or, we should add with some sadness, not connect at all).

The critic Harold Bloom has diagnosed the problem even more grimly. "I contemplate my many students," Bloom has written, "and I reflect on how many of them are Jewish in one way or another: confusedly, ambivalently, and partly. That is the way things are, the way they are going to be. What offers itself as normative Judaism does not speak to them, as it does not speak to me."[23] In place of "normative" Judaism—and midrash is clearly part of "normative" Judaism—Bloom offers the triad of Franz Kafka, Sigmund Freud, and Gershom Scholem as the contemporary canon of "high Jewish culture," of what he calls "Jewishness without Judaism."[24] But it is essentially Bloom's challenge to the "normative" tradition that every student of midrash must take seriously. Namely, can midrash speak to us today?

I would propose that it is precisely here that the midrash-theory connection can teach us: not by showing how to reclaim the substance of midrash or its methodology of reading, but by serving as a model for how theory can actively engage the classical "normative" tradition, and, once having engaged it, find the tradition more valuable and meaningful in its own right. For is the search for selfhood that led literary scholars to midrash so different in the end from the desire of laypersons to have these texts *do* something for them by revealing part of the mystery, the perplexity, of their existence as Jews? In both cases, what was and continues to be sought is a way to reclaim these texts for ourselves.

Ironically, Bloom's own early work in *Kabbalah and Criticism* might be instructive here as exemplifying the very process through which theory can participate in this act of recovery.[25] For while Bloom acknowledges that Kabbalah did not lead him to his theories of literary influence, there can be no question that Bloom gained his "feel" for Kabbalah—and his ability to communicate to his readers the palpable sense of the psychic energies that pulsate through those esoteric mystical bloodlines—from his knowledge of the history of post-Romantic poetry. His most brilliant intuition was to talk about Kabbalah as though it were poetry. And precisely because what he says about poetry is so compelling (at least to the reader initiated into the mysteries of Bloomian criticism), Bloom's travel guide to Kabbalah was able to afford access to its hidden paths through its revisionist, Gnostic, and Oedipal routes with an immediacy that has often eluded more conventional scholarship.

The questions that literary theory will raise when it turns to the tradition will concern "how deeply or feebly the tradition is reading its sources," as Geoffrey Hartman has aptly written.[26] Only by seeing how deeply the tradition reads its sources will we be able to learn to read the tradition deeply for ourselves. In this book I try to offer a model for how such questioning and reading might proceed so as to involve the tradition and ourselves in meaningful exchange. The book consists of four such exchanges on central topics in the study of midrash. Although it is not intended to be either an introduction to midrash for literary theorists or a primer in theory for midrash scholars, I have tried to write it in such a way that the book will be accessible *and* challenging to readers on both sides of the midrash-theory linkage, that is, sufficiently sophisticated to interest those with more training in either Rabbinics or literary theory and yet not so technical as to scare off scholars in one field who may be less familiar with the mysteries of the other.

The chapters in the book form a progression, but each one may also be read as an essay in its own right, which is indeed the way they were originally written and published. In preparing this book, I have revised the separate essays so as to knit them together into an extended discussion, but I have deliberately not attempted to do away with their essayistic nature. By calling these chapters essays, I mean, quite literally, that they are assays or attempts, that is, literary experiments in exploring an idea or text, in laying out the parameters of a problem, rather than more ambitious efforts aimed at resolving difficulties once and forever.

As a scholarly genre, the interpretive essay is a medium that, unfortunately, has not found a large place for itself in Jewish studies. In general, the field has favored either the scholarly article or the monograph, both of them more fitting vehicles for Wissenschaft, the "science" of Judaism, with its claims to precise and comprehensive knowledge. To be sure, authority and essayistic writing need not be exclusive. Gershom Scholem's great interpretive essays—"Revelation and Tradition as Religious Categories in Judaism," for example, or any of the essays in *Kabbalah and Its Symbolism*—are positive evidence to the contrary.[27] But the essay, by its very form, points in a different intellectual direction than the monograph—toward intellectual speculation and discovery rather than conclusive formulation and summary.

It would be presumptuous for any scholar to compare him- or herself to Scholem, but if the chapters in this book have any model, it is Scholem's great essays. Those essays, like the ones I have mentioned, epitomize scholarship that is, as George Steiner once wrote about Scholem's work, of "the life-giving kind."[28] Scholem's writing remains the most powerful testimony to the capacity of modern Jewish scholarship to transcend its secondary status as commentary on the classics of the past and to become a source of Jewish creativity in its own right—that is, to be able to embody the meaningfulness of Jewish tradition (even without necessarily subscribing to its content). To be sure, the power of Scholem's writing lay in many things: his magisterial learning and intelligence, his capacity for reconstructing the hidden myth at the heart of Kabbalistic doctrine, his genius for seeing the historical ramifications of these most arcane ideas in the farthest reaches of culture. But as sources to be read in their own right, perhaps the deepest measure of their power lay in the proven ability of Scholem's writings to inspire their readers—not to become Kabbalists themselves or to take up mystical beliefs and practices, but to go back to the tradition, to study its texts for themselves and, thereby, in some way, to partake of the power and fascination of Kabbalah on their own. If this book, too, can inspire only a few of its readers to read (or reread) midrash on their own, it will have more than justified its writing.

Chapter 1

Midrash and Hermeneutics: Polysemy vs. Indeterminacy

No questions have figured more prominently in the contemporary study of midrash than those of its hermeneutics. Is there a logic to interpretation in midrash, a set of rules or exegetical conventions governing the free play of its commentaries? Are those rules or their logic different from those of other interpretive traditions, and if so, what are those differences and what do they mean?

These questions are important not only because of what their answers might teach us about midrash. They also point to one of the primary reasons why midrash has fascinated students of literature and literary theory in general. Indeed, since that interest was first expressed some fifteen years ago, scholars have been trying to find in midrash an alternative to the various "logocentric" hermeneutical traditions, like that of allegoresis, that have dominated Western literary culture since antiquity. As a result, the urge to define the hermeneutics of midrash has been invested almost from the beginning with a desire to locate in Rabbinic exegesis a hermeneutic embodying Otherness.

This project has encountered many challenges. Among these, perhaps the most interesting has been the basic question that can be addressed to the entire post-structuralist project, and to deconstruction in particular: Is there "any other way that thinking may operate beyond or outside the enclosure of logocentrism?" This was precisely the question Zhang Longxi posed in a masterful study that explores the parallels between deconstruction and classical Chinese hermeneutics, a parallel that Jacques Derrida himself was among the first to invoke.[1] After subjecting Derrida's claims for the similarity of the two systems to the test of the Chinese perspective, Zhang disputes their validity, pointing out in the process a lengthy train of misinterpretations of Chinese thought by Western thinkers, among whom Derrida is only the most recent.

The deeper question raised by Zhang's argument, however, concerns the desire that led Derrida to invoke the Chinese model in the first place. That question, in turn, raises still other matters for inquiry, matters that in their broadest terms concern our every intellectual effort to look at non-Western culture through the lens of Western critical categories. If the essential theme of the Western hermeneutical tradition has been the challenge involved in understanding the Other, then cultures outside the West and their hermeneutical traditions would seem to epitomize Otherness. Yet granting that it is impossible for the subject (the interpreter) ever to achieve total identification with the object of interpretation (non-Western culture/its hermeneutical tradition/a document of interpretation in that tradition), how then does one proceed to understand the Other without distorting it in the very name of Otherness?

In dealing with cultures that have developed more or less independently of the West—like China or Africa, for example—the solutions to these methodological problems may more likely derive from literary anthropology than from pure theory.[2] The case of midrash raises still other considerations, however, since classical Rabbinic exegesis, like Rabbinic Judaism itself, was not so much completely "other" to, or apart from, Western culture as it was a marginal presence upon its borders, a tradition that developed by drawing upon Western categories and transforming them without becoming wholly absorbed by them. Historically, Rabbinic Judaism arose in late antiquity out of the fusion between ancient Near Eastern Israelite tradition and Hellenism. Not surprisingly, then, its literature, including midrash, borrowed from both the biblical and the classical literary traditions, yet managed to create for itself a fully distinct identity that exists in a kind of intermediate space between the conventional genres of Western literature.

Needless to say, any study of midrash must be able to encompass this complex historical etiology. No attempt will ever be sufficient that presents midrash and its hermeneutics in simple opposition to logocentrism, with the latter being characterized as a Greco-Roman or Christian development and the former as a Jewish one. To read midrash as a rewriting of Derrida, Jacques Lacan, or Edmond Jabès is equally misguided. The alternative, however, is not to study midrash through its own methods, which is essentially the way it has been read within traditional Jewish circles since the Middle Ages; rather, it is to approach midrash with a theoretical interest, fully prepared to take a stance toward literary theory roughly analogous to the marginal stance midrash (and Rabbinic Judaism) historically assumed in relation to the intellectual categories of Hellenism (and, in subsequent Jewish history, both Christianity and Islam), that is, simultaneously receptive and resistant to their universalist ambitions. Such an approach to midrash would be open to the categories of literary theory, yet conscious of *their* Otherness and ready to transform them by recontextualizing them.

In this chapter, I wish to investigate one aspect of midrash that has frequently been proposed as an antecedent or counterpart of the concept of indeterminacy as it has figured in post-structuralist literary theory, namely, its conception of Scriptural polysemy and its consequent habit of presenting multiple interpretations for Scriptural verses or phrases. As I hope to show, multiple interpretation in midrash bears little connection to the notion of indeterminacy; nonetheless, indeterminacy may still remain a significant category for understanding our reading of midrashic discourse. This lack of equivalence between midrash and the theoretical categories we use to read it may not be purely negative knowledge. Aside from the sheer antiquarian interest in understanding the midrashic phenomenon within its historical context, it may help us see a little more clearly the very conditions of our own theorizing.

Any consideration of the relationship between theory and midrash might do well to begin with the difference between the self-reflexivity of contemporary theory—thought turned in upon its own operations—and that of midrash, in which even theoretical statements about exegesis are couched in the language of Scriptural exegesis. No better example of the midrashic habit exists than the Rabbinic traditions about Scriptural polysemy. The locus classicus for these traditions is preserved in the Talmud, where they are cited in the course of a debate over the question as to whether or not one party may invoke multiple biblical verses in support of its position in a legal dispute, the assumption being that two prooftexts make a stronger case than one. Many sages appear to have opposed this practice, however, and accordingly the Talmud cites two sayings, the first attributed to Abbaye, a fourth-century Babylonian sage, and the second to the School of Rabbi Ishmael, a Palestinian sage who lived approximately two centuries earlier.

> Abbaye said: The verse says, "Once God has spoken, but twice I have heard" (Ps. 62:12). A single verse has several senses, but no two verses ever hold the same meaning.
>
> It was taught in the School of Rabbi Ishmael: "Behold, My word is like fire—declares the Lord—and like a hammer that shatters rock" (Jer. 23:29). Just as this hammer produces many sparks [when it strikes the rock], so a single verse has several meanings.[3]

Both of these interpretations make much the same point, but they derive it from separate verses in very different ways. The Psalms verse, which in its original context serves as an affirmation of God's faithfulness and justice, is understood by Abbaye as saying, in effect, "One thing God has spoken but two things I have heard," with the Hebrew words *ahat* and *shetayim* read not abverbially ("once" and "twice") but as substantives. In the case of the School of Rabbi Ishmael's saying, the verse from Jeremiah also has a meaning in its Scriptural context very different from the interpretation the sages give it. They understand Jeremiah's declaration as describing not the experience of prophecy but the substance of that experience, the content of prophetic revelation: specifically its literary product, the text of Scripture. This reading derives from what is for the Rabbis a genuine problem in the verse, namely, the presence of the two similes. The Rabbis always undertake their study of the Bible with the assumption that every word in Scripture is both necessary and significant. If this is so, however, why does the prophet use two similes for God's word, both fire *and* a hammer? The answer—in effect, the interpretation—given by the School of Rabbi Ishmael can be paraphrased as follows: My word, says God, is like fire; but what sort of fire? Like those fiery sparks produced by a hammer when it strikes rock—and like the many senses that every verse in Scripture holds ready to let fly at the strike of the interpretive hammer.[4]

The idea of Scriptural polysemy presented in these two sayings represents a virtual ideological cornerstone of midrashic exegesis. The concept does not appear to have changed or developed perceptibly through the classical Rabbinic period, and its use characterizes statements of both halakhah, Rabbinic law, and aggadah, the more homiletical and narrative portion of Rabbinic tradition. (If anything, polysemy is more frequent in aggadah than in halakhah.) Elsewhere in Rabbinic literature, the idea is expressed more allusively, often as a function of a stock number, usually seven or a multiple of seven. A statement in one midrash collection, Bamidbar (Numbers) Rabbah, thus refers to the seventy aspects (*panim*) of the Torah, while a later collection, *Mishnat Rabbi Eliezer,* refers to the forty-nine senses of Scripture. *The Alphabet of Rabbi Akiba,* a semimystical tract of the early post-Talmudic period, describes how Moses was instructed on Mount Sinai in "all seventy aspects of the seventy languages" of the Torah. This idea, however, is already suggested in the Talmud, in a passage that relates how on Mount Sinai "every commandment [*dibbur*] that went forth from the mouth of the Almighty was divided into seventy tongues."[5] As any student of midrash knows, the presentation of multiple interpretations (often, though not always, prefaced by the formula *davar aher*, "another interpretation") is its most ubiquitous feature, almost a kind of stereotype or commonplace.

The notion of Scriptural polysemy raises several questions: If every verse has several meanings, what did the Rabbis believe was the meaning of Scripture? Did the Bible even have a determinate sense for the Rabbis, or did they consider it essentially an open text, an unbounded field for the unlimited play of interpretation? If so, was any interpretation of Scripture valid? Or did there exist exegetical criteria, constraints upon the free activity of Scriptural interpretation, and if so, what were they? In the case of contradictory, mutually exclusive, or opposed exegeses, what criteria existed for resolving conflicts of interpretation?

We may begin by addressing the last question first, since it is explicitly discussed in the following passage, a homily attributed to another early sage of the second century, Rabbi Eleazar ben Azariah, as recorded in the Talmudic tractate Hagigah:

> [Rabbi Eleazar ben Azariah] recited this proem: "The words of the wise are like goads; like nails well-planted are the words of masters of assemblies; they were given by one shepherd" (Eccles. 12:11). Why are the words of the Torah likened to a goad? To teach you that just as the goad directs the heifer along its furrow to bring forth life to the world, so the words of the Torah direct those who study them from the paths of death to the paths of life. But [you might think that] just as the goad can move [and be removed], so the words of the Torah move [and can be removed]—therefore the text says: "nails" [which once nailed down cannot be removed]. But [you might think that] just as the nail only diminishes [as it is pounded into wood] and does not increase, so, too, the words of the Torah only diminish and do not increase—therefore the text says: "well-planted." Just as a plant grows and increases, so the words of Torah grow and increase. [What does the phrase] "the masters of assemblies" [mean?] These are the disciples of the wise who sit in assemblies and study the Torah, some pronouncing unclean and others pronouncing clean, some prohibiting and others permitting, some declaring unfit and others declaring fit. Should a man say: Since some pronounce unclean and others pronounce clean, some prohibit and others permit, some declare unfit and others declare fit—how then shall I learn Torah? Therefore Scripture says: All of them "were given from one shepherd." One God gave them, one leader (i.e., Moses) proclaimed them from the mouth of the Lord of all creation, blessed be He, as it is written, "And God spoke *all* these words" (Exod. 20:1 [my emphasis]). Therefore make your ear like the hopper and acquire a perceptive heart to understand the words of those who pronounce unclean and the words of those who pronounce clean, the words of those who prohibit and the words of those who permit, the words of those who declare unfit and the words of those who declare fit.[6]

This passage is a proem, or *petihta*, a common midrashic literary form that probably derived from brief sermons delivered in the synagogue immediately before the weekly reading from Scripture. We will discuss this form in greater detail in chapter 3. For now we need only say that the structure of the proem is highly conventional: it nearly always concludes with the initial verse in the weekly reading (here, Exod. 20:1), and virtually always opens with a verse taken from a completely different and unrelated context in Scripture (here, Eccles. 12:11). After citing this latter verse, the preacher interprets it in such a way as to build a connection or bridge to the concluding verse. Because the audience knows that verse in advance, the rhetorical shape of the form largely depends upon the unpredictability and virtuousity with which the preacher can make the connection between the two verses.

In this proem, Rabbi Eleazar ben Azariah's interpretation of Eccles. 12:11 offers an almost perfect illustration of midrashic reading. In the first place, the sage never has any doubt about the overall sense of the verse: "the words of the wise" can refer only to the teachings of the sages themselves. The exegete's task therefore does not involve disclosing a less obvious, hidden, or revisionist meaning for the verse; rather, it consists of unpacking the significance of each separate simile or phrase in the verse. That significance, characteristically, is assumed to lie in a substantive contribution to meaning, not in figurative or ornamental novelty.

To unpack these points of significance, Rabbi Eleazar begins by "atomizing" the verse, interpreting each phrase as an independent hermeneutical item. Atomization, one of the most common exegetical techniques of midrash, proceeds from the assumption that every word and phrase in Scripture is as meaningful in itself as within its larger Scriptural context. Yet with each successive attempt to fix a meaning for the separate phrases, Rabbi Eleazar finds himself faced by an alternative meaning or implication that threatens to undo the interpretation he has just proposed. If the words of the Torah are truly like a goad on a beast of burden's neck, perhaps they, too, can be removed? To resolve this hermeneutical dilemma, Rabbi Eleazar uses another common midrashic technique: he revises his initial interpretation by interpreting Scripture through Scripture. In this passage, he does so by modifying the initial figure with the succeeding phrase in the verse, the following simile or figure. Thus, he is able to rebut the unforeseen and problematic implication of his previous interpretation likening Torah to a goad by invoking the next figure in the verse, in which the words of the wise are compared to nails, permanently and unalterably fixed. Following this revision, however, Rabbi Eleazar faces still another objection. If the words of Torah are like nails, do they also diminish (as they disappear into the wood into which they are hammered)? No: for they are like plants; they grow and increase. And so on.

In its overall sequence, this chain of interpretations suggests a unified or univocal reading of Scripture rather than a truly polysemous one. In typical Rabbinic fashion, though, the very next interpretation in the passage offers an explicit formulation of polysemy. This is Rabbi Eleazar's interpretation for the phrase "the masters of assemblies," which he takes as a reference to the sages themselves as they study and debate the law—some pronouncing unclean, others clean; some prohibiting, others permitting; and so on. If this indeed is the case, the passage continues, a student might wonder, "How then can I learn Torah?" Rabbi Eleazar responds: There is no cause for despair. Although the sages' opinions may contradict each other, they all are part of Torah, part of a single revelation. They all were once spoken by the mouth of one shepherd, Moses, who in turn received them all from one God. Rabbi Eleazar's confirmation for this answer lies in the exegesis he offers for Exod. 20:1, the verse that serves as the introduction to the revelation at Sinai in which God gave the Ten Commandments—the basis of the complete Torah—to the children of Israel.[7]

It should be noted that the student's question is *not* "How can I practice the law?" The answer to that question would be clear to any disciple of the Rabbis: where there is a difference of opinion regarding the correct law, the halakhah is decided by following the opinion of the majority of sages, a principle of jurisprudence the Rabbis elsewhere justify midrashically through an interpretation of Exod. 23:2, "after the majority incline."[8] Rather than point to a practical quandary, the student's question and the hermeneutical despair underlying it derive from the chaos of the academy: If the Rabbis disagree about the meaning of every law and verse, if each and every law and verse can elicit opposite interpretations simultaneously, then why bother to study Torah?

This dilemma recalls still another passage, the famous description of the first-century schools or "houses" of Hillel and Shammai, named after the legendary Pharisaic sages. The two schools are typically remembered in Rabbinic tradition as engaging in endless debates:

> Rabbi Abba said in the name of Samuel: For three years the House of Hillel and the House of Shammai argued. These said, The law is according to our view; and the others said, The law is according to our view. [Finally] a heavenly oracle decreed: The words of both houses are the words of the living God, and the law is like the House of Hillel.

The Talmud then asks, quite reasonably:

> But if the words of both houses are the words of the living God, why did the House of Hillel merit having the halakhah decided according to its view? Because they were peaceful and humble men, and they taught the teachings of the House of Shammai as well as their own, and even more than that, they taught the teachings of the House of Shammai before they taught their own.[9]

In other words, the halakhah was eventually decided according to the opinion of the House of Hillel not because its teachings were any more correct or valid than those of the House of Shammai, but for ethical reasons. Even though the House of Hillel disagreed with its opponents, it treated the House of Shammai with respect. Another tradition tells us that while the Houses of Hillel and Shammai disagreed over the legitimacy of children born from certain types of marriages, they still did not refrain from marrying each others' daughters—because, we are told, they preferred to practice the Scriptural command, "You must love truth and peace" (Zech. 8:19).[10] From a strictly hermeneutical perspective, however, both interpretations, even if they contradict each other, are considered equally true, identically alive to Torah's meaning, to the words of the living God.

The sanction for such paradoxical truth is explicitly stated in the homily of Rabbi Eleazar: it is the divine origins that both interpretations are said to share, the belief that the contradictory opinions of the two houses were both originally spoken by the mouth of the Lord of all creation. This divine sanction for Scriptural polysemy also differentiates the midrashic concept of polysemy from its post-structuralist counterpart, indeterminacy. By indeterminacy, I hasten to add, I do not mean nihilism, the sheer relativizing or negation of meaning as an infinitely deferred presence, or nonpresence. Instead, I refer to the concept as it has been subtly characterized by Geoffrey Hartman, as being close to the process of commentary itself, "the taking away, modification, elaboration of previous meanings."[11] In this sense, midrashic reading can sometimes be, as in Rabbi Eleazar's interpretation of Eccles. 12:11, very close to a literary criticism predicated on indeterminacy. What differentiates midrash from indeterminacy is not its style but rather the latter's formal resistance to closure, its final revelation of a perspective that, as Hartman writes, "may be, precisely, the absence of one and only one context from which to view the flux of time or the empirical world, of one and only one method that would destabilize all but itself, of one and only one language to rule understanding and prevent misunderstanding."[12] In contrast, midrashic polysemy is predicated precisely upon the existence of such a perspective, the divine presence from which all contradictory interpretations derive. Precisely what type of perspective this is we will try to say shortly.

The difference between Rabbinic polysemy and contemporary indeterminacy is fairly clear. What is more instructive, however, is the fact that the midrashic conception has no real parallel, so far as I know, even in other interpretive traditions in the ancient world that also approached the Bible as a divinely inspired text. Consider the example of the earliest datable literature of Jewish biblical exegesis, the fragments of commentaries found among the Dead Sea Scrolls at Qumran. The technical term for exegesis at Qumran is *pesher*, a Hebrew word cognate to the Sumerian *bur* and the Akkadian *pasharu*, verbal roots that mean "to release, resolve, and solve," and that became in ancient Near Eastern dream-interpretation literature the technical terms for the therapeutic-magical process whereby the symbolic meaning of a dream—particularly of a troubling dream—is explained, and hence explained away.[13] In the Bible, a cognate verb, *patar*, is also used for dream interpretation, and the same root, as we shall see, is the basis for the name of a specific type of midrashic interpretation, the *petirah*.[14]

The connection between Qumranic pesher and ancient dream interpretation is a virtual commonplace of modern scholarship.[15] Like ancient dream interpretation, with its singleminded desire to unravel the one and only meaning of the dream, pesher interpretation views Scripture as an enigma to be solved and decoded. The key to the solution, its underlying code, is the apocalyptic history of the sectarian Dead Sea community itself. Thus, in the Pesher Habakkuk, one phrase after another in the book of Habakkuk is made to refer to a contemporary event or personage, from the Teacher of Righteousness (as the founder of the sect appears to have been known) and his followers to their many and assorted Jewish enemies, as well as to Rome, the Gentile scourge. In this exegesis there is little room for contradictory or multiple interpretations.[16] Indeed, the apocalyptic force of the commentary, its persuasiveness as a political and religious document, depends directly on the absoluteness of its claim that each and every interpretation is true and that the contemporary meanings—the events and personages—that underlie the Scriptural text will exhaust that text's prophecy as soon as they come to pass in the imminent future. The same type of interpretation appears as well in the New Testament Gospels, in the so-called fulfillment prophecies in which verses from the Hebrew Bible are cited as prophecies of events that are said to have been realized in the life of Jesus. The most famous of these prophecies is Matthew's misinterpretation of Isa. 7:14, "the maiden is with child and will soon give birth to a son whom she will call Immanuel," which Matthew understood as a prophecy fulfilled in the virgin birth.

As in Qumranic exegesis, many exegetical techniques in Rabbinic midrash can also be traced to various procedures of ancient dream interpretation.[17] Yet the essential thrust of midrash toward finding multiple interpretations of Scripture could not be more opposed to the basic intentions of ancient dream interpretation. Unlike the exegetes of Qumran, the Rabbis appear to have repudiated the absolutist claims of apocalyptic fulfillment in favor of hermeneutical multiplicity. For example, the petirah, the cognate midrashic form I have mentioned, adapts for midrash the form of the Qumranic pesher. Like the pesher, the petirah takes an ahistorical, generally abstract if not abstruse biblical verse, and applies it to a concrete and specific event. Unlike the pesher, however, the events interpreted in the petirah are not contemporary, certainly not imminent in the eschatological future (or recent, near apocalyptic past, as in the New Testament use of the fulfillment form); rather, they tend to be chosen from the distant past, usually from the biblical past, a realm of history that can be characterized best by its unthreatening distance from the interpreter. Furthermore, once again in contrast to Qumranic pesher, midrashic petirot, even when they are applied to the biblical narrative, are usually presented in series—not just one petirah, but two or three, sometimes as many as four or five.[18] The apocalyptic and absolutist claims of Qumranic pesher have effectively been neutralized in midrash—in the religious-political as well as in the hermeneutical sphere—by a virtually ideological policy of polysemy.

Similarly, there are no real parallels to multiple interpretations of the midrashic sort in the various hermeneutical traditions of the classical and early Christian worlds. Classical allegoresis developed as an apologetic instrument of Stoic and Neoplatonic rationalizers of Homeric myth, and it was later utilized by Philo as a technique for the philosophical interpretation of Scripture. From its beginnings, allegory distinguished between and built upon two distinct levels of meaning: first, the literal or manifest meaning (*to phaneron*); second, the underlying or deeper sense (*hē huponoia*). As early as Philo, however, this second level began to be subdivided into more subtle categories—the naturalistic, the ethical, the metaphysical or mystical—and these three subcategories eventually developed in medieval Christian exegesis into the famous fourfold senses of Scripture.

Yet while these traditions all seem to predicate multiple interpretation as a condition of exegesis, the different senses they find in Scripture actually represent a hierarchy of meanings rather than a truly polysemous range of interpretations, each one separate from the others. The medieval senses, rather than being distinct hermeneutical categories, are more like levels of interpretation that could in fact be ordered in an ascending ladder of significance.[19] This is very different from the multiple interpretations of Scripture found in midrash. For example, Hab. 1:7, "That one is terrible, dreadful; its laws and majesty proceed from itself," a verse that in its original context refers to the Chaldeans, is interpreted in Vayikra (Leviticus) Rabbah 18:2 six different ways. According to the midrash, it refers, respectively, to Adam, Esau, Sennacharib, Hiram King of Tyre, Nebuchadnezzar, and the Israelites! Even if the interpretations relating to Esau, Sennacharib, Hiram, and Nebuchadnezzar all might be said to be versions of a single interpretive prototype—to refer to an enemy of God (as the first half of the verse is in effect interpreted) from whom a faithful servant of God eventually descended (as the second half of the verse is understood)—one could hardly use this categorization for the interpretations referring to Adam and to the Israelites. These two opinions do not even parallel each other. Or to give another example: on Lam. 3:10, "He is a lurking bear to me," a reference to the unnamed and cruel enemy who is torturing the speaker (an anonymous male personifying the nation of Israel), Eikhah (Lamentations) Rabbah offers two opinions regarding his historical identity. According to one, the bear is God; according to the other, it is Vespasian (the Roman general and emperor to whom the Rabbis attributed the major blame for the destruction of the Temple in 70 C.E.). This last pair of interpretations represents the aggadic equivalent to the opposed interpretations of the Houses of Hillel and Shammai in the realm of halakhah.

The closest analogue to midrashic polysemy that one can find in the Church Fathers is in Augustine. In one of the most inspired exegeses in the entire history of Scriptural interpretation, Augustine reads God's blessing to mankind "to be fruitful and multiply" (Gen. 1:22, 28) as an injunction to multiply interpretations of Scripture, "to express in manifold ways what we understand in but one, and to understand in manifold ways what we read as obscurely uttered in but one way."[20]

And certainly no medieval exegete delights more than Augustine does in multiple interpretations. For Gen. 1:1 alone he offers five different readings.[21]

Yet, even for Augustine, the possibility of multiple interpretations in Scriptural exegesis is less a function of an inherently polysemous sacred text than it is the result of the biblical author's own obscurity. That obscurity may possess divine sanction, but its presence nonetheless creates a hermeneutical dilemma for the biblical exegete, making it impossible for him or her to determine the originally intended meaning of a verse, and thereby leading the interpreter to invent other readings. For Augustine, however, this eventuality is not inherently dangerous so long as those other meanings represent the "truth" and are "congruous with the truth taught in other passages of the Holy Scriptures."[22] By truth Augustine essentially means *caritas*, that "love of a Being which is to be enjoyed and of a being that can share that enjoyment with us," which serves him as a near rule of faith. While Augustine did not invent the rule of faith, he seems to have been among the first to use it to justify (rather than to prohibit) exegetical innovation. A person who understands Scripture in a way different from that intended by its author may therefore be deceived, but "if he is deceived in an interpretation which builds up *caritas*, which is the end of the commandments, he is deceived in the same way as a man who leaves a road by mistake but passes through a field to the same place towards which the road itself leads."[23]

To be sure, one could argue that Rabbinic Judaism also possesses a "rule of faith" under which all multiple interpretations are to be subsumed. The problem, however, is in stipulating in what this rule consists. If all the statements about faith that characterize Rabbinic Judaism were collected, they would more closely resemble the anthologies of multiple interpretations for a single verse that are found in Rabbinic exegesis than a systematic exposition of religious beliefs. This feature of Rabbinic thought has led one modern Jewish theologian to describe its condition as "the indeterminacy of belief."[24] At least since the time of Maimonides, Jewish philosophers have been aware of the Rabbis' apparent lack of interest in making a theologically coherent whole out of their disparate articles of faith. Only in the recent past, in fact, has the absence of a systematic theology come to be viewed as a virtue of Rabbinic Judaism rather than as a failure.

Those attempting to describe institutional controls on interpretation within the Rabbinic community face difficulties analogous to those seeking to define a rule of faith for Rabbinic Judaism. Such controls surely must have existed. Yet outside of the most obviously impossible cases—a reading of Isa. 7:14 as a prophecy of the virgin birth of Jesus as messiah—it is difficult to say precisely what lay beyond the borders of discourse. To be certain, most institutional controls work silently through what Frank Kermode has described as "the tacit knowledge of the permitted range of sense."[25] Indeed, the literature of Rabbinic Judaism sometimes seems to have been edited almost intentionally to camouflage any institutional constraints or conflicts. Yet while Rabbinic literature is replete with controversies and disagreements between Rabbis (one Rabbi may even accuse another of distorting the sense of Scripture), the fact remains that the objectionable or disputed interpretation is usually preserved within the Rabbinic corpus together with the unobjectionable or authoritative exegesis; both are handed down as equal words of the living God.[26] There is little evidence to support the existence of explicit mechanisms for internal censorship in Rabbinic society.[27]

Even so, the absence of a rule of faith in Rabbinic Judaism, or the impossibility of determining the institutional forces that may have controlled exegesis, does not mean that midrash was ever entirely open or unconstrained. For one thing, there appear to have existed schools of exegesis with distinct hermeneutical approaches or tendencies. There also existed "lists" of hermeneutical rules and exegetical techniques that reflect some awareness of the mechanisms of interpretation. These lists, however, were not composed to serve as how-to manuals for "doing" midrash; rather, scholars of Rabbinics today believe that they were more likely compiled at comparatively late dates by specific exegetical schools to legitimate their hermeneutical methods and to provide polemical documentation against competing exegetical schools (or competing religious groups, like the Karaite sect in the early Middle Ages).[28] In practice, Rabbinic exegesis also turns out to be far less polysemous than some statements we have seen might lead us to expect. Many multiple interpretations, like the exegeses for Hab. 1:7 cited earlier, are actually versions of the same idea and recur in different contexts. Furthermore, while midrash may be unsystematic, its exegeses are not unmotivated. Even at its most apparently far-fetched or flamboyant moments, midrashic interpretations tend to be situated on genuine textual cruces or irregularities, "bumps" in the plain surface of Scripture, a fact that militates against the worst excesses of unbridled polysemy. Finally, there appears to be a kind of underlying "deep structure" in midrash that both produces and governs multiple interpretations under specific exegetical conditions. This deep structure, as Betty Roitman has recently argued, "enacts at the level of interpretation a dialectic formulated on the ontological plane by Rabbi Akiba: 'All is foreseen, but freedom of choice is given.'" In midrash, Roitman writes, "all is determined, and yet all is open."[29]

Roitman's theologized formulation suggests a possible direction in which to look for a model or explanation for the concept of polysemy in midrash. In contemporary criticism, textual meaning is often described spatially, in terms of its position either "behind" the text (the traditional logocentric view) or "in front" of it (from the perspective of deconstruction). In the case of Rabbinic Judaism, the divine guarantee of meaning in Scripture might be described more accurately as coming from above, not in the sense of divine effluence or emanation but literally from on high, from the top of Mount Sinai, where, the Rabbis claimed, God gave Moses not only Scripture, "the written Torah" or the Pentateuch, but also an "oral Torah," passed on by mouth from generation to generation. That oral Torah effectively comprised everything in Rabbinic Judaism not explicitly stated in the written Torah. As revealed in its totality at Sinai, it included every multiple interpretation of Scripture, including, as one celebrated saying states, "the very words a disciple of the sages will speak before his teacher."[30]

The two aspects of Torah, written and oral, are not exactly equivalent for the Rabbis, but together they form a unified, timeless entity with a single origin in the divine revelation. As we have already seen, certain Rabbinic traditions, like those describing every divine utterance at Sinai as having been issued in seventy tongues, seem to connect polysemy with the original revelation. Other traditions that describe God's external appearance at different moments when He manifested Himself to Israel have a family resemblance to the traditions about the polysemous meaning of Torah. Thus, in one famous passage, we are told that

> God appeared to [the children of Israel] at the Red Sea like a hero in battle, at Sinai like a scribe instructing them in Torah, and in the days of Daniel like an elderly teacher. [God] said to them: Just because you see Me in many images, this does not mean that there are many gods. . . . Said Rabbi Hanina bar Papa: God appeared to them with an angry face, with a neutral face, with a pleasant expression, and with a smiling face. Said Rabbi Levi: God appeared to them like a statue which looks in every direction. A thousand people look at it, and it looks at each of them. Thus, when God spoke to Israel, each Jew said: it is to me that the voice is speaking.[31]

Just as a single verse may have many meanings, so God, too, is said to possess many countenances.

A more explicit treatment of the connection between God and the Torah can be found in the following passage in Bereshit Rabbah, the midrash on the book of Genesis. The passage below, attributed to Rabbi Hoshaya, is the very first interpretation in the collection. Although its subject is Gen. 1:1, it begins with a series of interpretations of Prov. 8:30, a verse that in its original context is spoken by Wisdom, an allegorical figure that the Rabbis identified with Torah:

> Rabbi Hoshaya began: "I was with Him as an *amon* [Translated in the Jewish Publication Society TaNaKh as "a confidant"; in the Jerusalem Bible as "a master craftsman"], a source of delight every day, rejoicing before Him at all times" (Prov. 8:30). The word *amon* means a tutor. *Amon* means "covered." *Amon* means "hidden." And some say it means "great." [Each of these interpretations is based on a phonetic pun between the word *amon* and another, similar-sounding word; verses from Scripture to support each interpretation are then cited for all four opinions.] Another interpretation: *amon* means an artisan.

> The Torah declares: I was the instrument that the Holy One, blessed be He, used when He practiced His craft. It is customary that when a king of flesh and blood builds a palace, he doesn't build it himself but he hires an architect; even the architect doesn't build it solely from his head, but he uses plans and blueprints in order to know how to lay the rooms and to arrange the doors. So, too, the Holy One, blessed be He, looked into the Torah and created the world. And so the Torah said: "By means of [*be-*, a particle conventionally translated as "in"] the beginning, God created the heavens and the earth," and the word "beginning" always alludes to the Torah, as Scripture says, "The Lord created me at the beginning of His course" (Prov. 8:22).[32]

The word *amon* in the Proverbs verse happens to be a *hapax legomenon*, a fact that helps to explain Rabbi Hoshaya's puzzlement at its meaning and why so many interpretations are offered for it. Yet these multiple interpretations also exemplify the kind of wit one typically finds in midrash; indeed, in the second half of the opening Proverbs verse, Torah (Wisdom) is itself described explicitly in terms of this wit as God's constant joy and delight, something that entertains Him all day. As an interpretive activity, midrash is a form of study that is also an avenue of entertainment, playful and serious at once. Thus, all four interpretations of *amon* are based on ingenious if contrived puns. Yet each interpretation also presents a different conception of the Torah. One of these—the definition of *amon* as a tutor, a *pidagog*—may even allude polemically to a Christian doctrine. It recalls Paul's famous characterization of the law in Gal. 3:24 as a *paidagogos* whom God appointed over the Israelites, that is, a teacher or schoolmaster whose role, after the crucifixion, was superseded by faith in Christ as a means of justification.[33] Such multiple motivations for a single exegetical impulse are highly typical of midrash.

For our present purposes, the most revealing exegesis in the passage is the final interpretation of *amon* as the blueprint, the plan, that God used in creating the universe. Although the Torah is described here as though it existed before the creation of the world, like the Logos, the idea is not necessarily Platonic.[34] The Torah is not being defined as the idea whose second-order reflection is the universe; rather, the Torah is conceived as the instrument God used in creating the world, as His blueprint and set of directions, which He looks into the way an architect looks into a blueprint, or the way the Rabbis themselves looked into the Torah as the blueprint for the existence they constructed for themselves. Torah, then, is not identical with God; its relationship to Him is, one might say, metonymic rather than metaphoric, a matter of extension rather than resemblance. The study of Torah, the activity of midrash, does not therefore constitute an act of directly interpreting God as though the text itself were literally divine. Instead, one could almost call midrash the interpretation of Torah as a figure or trope standing for God.

The concept of Torah in midrash can therefore be characterized best by its figurative status. As in all cases of rhetorical figuration, this status allows the Torah to be both identified and not identified with its presumed object. To begin with the positive side, the near identification of Torah and God provides the Rabbis with the basic axioms of midrashic hermeneutics: first, the belief in the omnisignificance of Scripture, in the meaningfulness of its every word, letter, even (according to one famous report) scribal flourish; second, the claim of the essential unity of Scripture as the expression of the single divine will. From the first axiom proceeds the common midrashic technique of atomization, whereby verses and phrases, sometimes even single words, in Scripture are broken up into smaller units, which are then exploited in isolation for hermeneutical significance. From the second axiom derives the equally typical midrashic habit of viewing the Bible atemporally, of explaining Scripture through Scripture, and of connecting the most disparate and seemingly unrelated verses in order to create new and overreaching nexuses of meaning: in short, intertextuality that is elevated in midrash to the level of a virtual exegetical principle.

Both hermeneutical axioms and their resulting practices stem from the association of Torah with its author—or, as in the midrash cited earlier, of the blueprint with the architect, who presumably drew the blueprint to help him in his job. To know Torah, to read and follow the divine blueprint, is, in this sense, a way to come to know the mind of the divine architect, and ultimately, to imitate Him and construct a human existence modeled after God's creation of the world. From this perspective it is possible to understand why midrash is not merely an act of literary interpretation but a path toward holiness. "If you want to come to know the One who spoke and created the world, study [midrash] aggadah," the Rabbis said, "and you will come to know Him who by His word created the world." As Judah Goldin has recently argued, this seemingly theological axiom may actually be a polemical statement asserting that one can serve God through the study of aggadah and through midrash as effectively as by the practice of halakhah.[35]

The other side of the equation between God and Torah, however, is the refusal of midrash to make the identification of Torah and God literal. This side can easily be seen if one compares the midrashic position with mystical, quasi-Gnostic conceptions of Torah as the name of God and of Scriptural exegesis as the unfolding of the essence of that name. The full identification of Torah with God becomes truly explicit only in the kabbalistic speculation of the later Middle Ages, in formulations that openly connect the infinity of God's being with the infinity of meanings to be found in Torah, and in Scriptural exegesis that "decodes the Bible as a mystical biography of the infra-divine infinite processes and the regulations which influence the function of those processes."[36] Yet even in the Rabbinic period, there are testimonies in contemporary mystical/Gnostic documents that literally identify God and Torah: one hymn refers to the text of the Torah as being inscribed upon

God's "limbs," his "arms" and "legs."[37] Other texts, using similarly anthropomorphic terms, speak of Scriptural interpretation as literal description of God's body. This notion of Torah is clearly different from the one underlying midrash; indeed, midrash might even be said to have denied this equation. A midrashic exegesis always returns to the text, not to God.

Just as midrash rejects the mystical idea of the literal infinity of meanings in the Torah (and its corollary, the infinity of God), so, too, does midrash avoid the twin conceptions of the interpreter as a transported, divinely inspired being and of the act of interpretation as a mantic, prophetic activity occuring within states of ecstacy, through paranormal spiritual experiences—angelic revelations, daemonic encounters, oneiric messages, and so on. For the mystical conception of interpretation, such experiences are virtually a "condition for the attainment of the sublime secrets of Torah."[38] As the distance between God and Torah disappears, the distinction between God and man becomes equally blurred, so that the mystical act of inspired interpretation itself becomes an occasion for *unio mystica*.

Descriptions of supernatural phenomena attending sages engaged in Scriptural interpretation are not entirely lacking in Rabbinic literature.[39] But the act of interpretation in midrash is itself almost completely severed from any connection with prophecy or analogous types of revelatory experience. One of the most famous stories in all Rabbinic literature relates how one sage, Rabbi Eliezer ben Hyrkanus, disputed with the entire academy of sages at Yavneh over a matter concerning the laws of purity. Refusing to concede his position, Rabbi Eliezer called upon heaven to come to his aid and testify on his behalf. Immediately, the story relates, Rabbi Eliezer successfully ordered a carob tree to uproot itself and fly a hundred feet (according to some, four hundred feet); then, for a nearby stream to flow backward; finally, for a divine oracle to confirm his position. Nevertheless, the sages refused to accept the divine testimony, citing as proof of their own position—as decided by majority rule—the Deuteronomic verse, "It is not in heaven" (Deut. 3:12), which Rabbi Yermiyah interpreted as follows: "Since the Torah has already been given from Mount Sinai, we do not pay attention to heavenly voices, for You have already written at Mount Sinai, 'after the majority incline' (Exod. 23:2)." Rabbi Yermiyah effectively invokes Scripture against God. The story concludes by relating how God, listening in heaven to this Rabbinic debate, laughed and said, "My children have defeated me, my children have defeated me!"[40]

The dissociation of interpretation from prophecy also distinguishes midrashic exegesis from other types of Scriptural exegesis more contemporary with the Rabbis. As Joseph Blenkinsopp has shown, the transition from prophecy to interpretation as a source of religious authority was initially achieved by attributing prophetic inspiration to interpretation.[41] This move can be witnessed as early as in the book of Daniel, but it is far more evident in the most famous example of biblical exegesis found at Qumran, the Pesher Commentary on Habakkuk.

This commentary not only attributes prophetic stature to its interpreter-author, possibly the Teacher of Righteousness himself; it even claims, as part of its exegesis of Habakkuk, that the prophet Habakkuk wrote down the prophecies God had revealed to him without knowing the meaning of what he wrote. Indeed, God is said to have concealed that meaning until the Teacher of Righteousness was born and "God made known [to him] all the mysteries of the words of His servants the Prophets."[42] This last claim is itself derived from a phrase in Habakkuk, "that he who reads may read it speedily" (Hab. 2:2). According to the pesher interpretation of this phrase, God in effect foresees that the prophet-interpreter will supersede the prophet-writer in prophetic power and will usurp his position.

Viewed against the backdrop of Qumranic exegesis, it is possible to see in midrash an attempt on the part of the Rabbis to divest exegesis of both such prophetic pretensions (and their potential subversion of Scripture's unique status) and the more publicly dangerous charge of apocalyptic and sectarian politics. To be sure, this act of repudiation—or neutralization, if you wish—also expressed an agenda of its own. The destruction of the Temple in 70 C.E. and the catastrophes that followed in subsequent centuries bred in the Rabbis a certain despair with history, as it did in many of their contemporaries, but that despair did not lead them into either apocalyptic fantasy or Gnostic dualism. Rather, the estrangement that the Rabbis felt had developed between God and the world, the disparity they saw between the divine promise and its fulfillment in human reality, appears to have turned their energies inward, into the construction of paradigms of holiness within their self-enclosed society. Seemingly oblivious to the larger historical arena in which they lived, yet wary as well of their own desire for messianically inspired political activism, they instead directed their imaginations toward the text of the Torah and its interpretation.

The Rabbis' conception of Torah as a figurative trope for God—treating God and Torah simultaneously as identical and not identical—expresses both their sense of alienation and their attempt to overcome that alienation intellectually. Following the destruction of the Temple, the text of the Torah became for the Rabbis the primary sign of the continued existence of the covenantal relationship between God and Israel, and the activity of Torah study—midrash—thus became the foremost medium for preserving and pursuing that relationship. Understood this way, the object of midrash was not so much to find the meaning of Scripture as it was literally to engage its text. Midrash became a kind of conversation the Rabbis invented in order to enable God to speak to them from between the lines of Scripture, in the textual fissures and discontinuities that exegesis discovers. The multiplication of interpretations in midrash was one way, as it were, to prolong that conversation.

To some extent, Rabbinic exegesis, like the interpretive ideologies of Western culture, is motivated by an anxiety about the loss of meaning or presence (an anxiety that has led Western thinkers to substitute for genuine presence a metaphysics of presence or, as Derrida has argued, a covert theology)—hence the ubiquitous concern of midrash to prove the relevance of Torah to every conceivable circumstance, to make it embrace every aspect of life. But more than fearing that the divine guarantee behind Scripture's meaning may have been lost, the Rabbis were haunted by the worry, the deeper fear, that *their* tradition of interpretation, the entire body of practice and exegesis expressed in the oral Torah, may *not* have represented the authoritative, the one and only divinely sanctioned heritage of the biblical revelation.

Part of this anxiety derived from the Rabbis' historical experience. Palestinian Judaism in late antiquity consisted of a spectrum of competing religious sects—among them the Qumran sects, the Jewish Christians, the Rabbis themselves (or their predecessors, like the Pharisees)—each of which claimed to be the sole and authentic heir of the biblical tradition. Among these groups, the Rabbis were not always the most obviously successful (nor the least), but the destruction of the Temple in 70 C.E. was exploited by some of their competitors (Christians, for example) to prove that God had rejected the Jews and chosen others, like themselves, as the true Israel. Yet even without such specific provocations, the Rabbis' anxiety over their election was in some sense inevitable. It was bound to have arisen since, after all, Rabbinic Judaism, like other Jewish sects of the period, *was* an extension of biblical religion, not identical with it, and it was not the only such adumbration of that heritage or the only interpretation of the Bible's contemporary relevance.

The response the Rabbis made to these doubts about their election, about the authority of their tradition, was to adopt an interpretive posture that represents the very opposite of Harold Bloom's idea of the anxiety of influence. The Rabbis consciously—happily, we might say—assume the stance of belatedness. Precisely what they seek to prove is that all the innovations and inventions of their tradition can already be found in the text of the Bible, that nothing they say is original; hence the essential preoccupation of midrash with finding in the biblical text a source for every law and belief in Rabbinic tradition, no matter how contrived the connection may be. Thus, too, the Rabbis' overriding concern with confirming the chain of tradition, a chain they claim began with God's revelation at Sinai and proceeded, oral link by link, from Moses and the prophets down through the generations to Ezra and finally to the sages themselves. And finally, this same anxiety is doubtless the source for the virtual obsession in Rabbinic discourse with attribution, with naming authors and tradents and tracing the history of traditions. A student who neglects to name the author of a tradition will forget all his learning one tradition reports by way of warning.[43] Given all the special exigencies of their historical situation, it is not difficult to understand the essential conservatism of the Rabbis, their upholding of tradition and refusal of prophecy as well as anything else that might be construed as usurpation of Scripture's unique status.

Such contented belatedness was one way the Rabbis expressed their anxiety over the claim to being the sole authentic heirs of the biblical tradition. Another response, perhaps more pertinent to their interpretive activities, can be seen in their treatment of multiple interpretations. The question asked by Rabbi Eleazar's student—"How can I study Torah?"—may also be understood as an expression of anxiety. If the Rabbis disagree about every point of the law, if they cannot even agree among themselves about its meaning, then how can they claim to be its genuine interpreters, the owners of its truth? One response is given by Rabbi Eleazar: even in the case of conflicts, the opinions of both sages—the one who permits and the one who forbids—are the words of the living God.

From this perspective, the citation of multiple interpretations in midrash is an attempt to represent in textual terms an idealized academy of Rabbinic tradition where all the opinions of the sages are recorded equally as part of a single divine conversation. Opinions that in human discourse may appear contradictory or mutually exclusive are raised to the state of paradox once traced to their common source in the speech of the divine author.

This representation, however, is a literary artifact. Like much of Rabbinic discourse, it attempts to capture or to imitate in writing the oral exchanges that took place between sages both in formal debates in the academy and on less formal occasions elsewhere. The phenomenon we witness in multiple interpretation, in other words, is in actuality a literary impression, something of an illusion created by the redaction of Rabbinic literature, the result of a common choice made by its anonymous editors to preserve minority as well as majority opinions, the varieties of traditions rather than single versions. In making this choice, the Rabbinic editors did not act without precedent; indeed, they followed in a venerable tradition of early Jewish literature that included such other sacred "compromise texts" as the Pentateuch, in which separate documentary sources are combined into a single composition as though their agendas and ideologies were compatible (which they eventually were made out to be), or the New Testament, in which the four Gospels, each with a different Christology, stand side by side.[44] The difference between these earlier texts and the Rabbinic midrashim is simply that in the latter editorial policy was elevated to the order of exegetical ideology, that is, polysemy functions as a trait of sacred Scripture. Here, for the first time, editorial pluralism has become a condition of meaning.

Polysemy in midrash, then, is to be understood as a claim to textual stability rather than its opposite, an indeterminate state of endlessly deferred meanings and unresolved conficts. In fact, midrashic polysemy suggests more than just textual stability; it points to a fantasy of social stability, of human community in complete harmony, where disagreement is either resolved agreeably or maintained peacefully. Such a fantasy of inner oneness, beyond difference, would certainly have counterbalanced the Rabbis' sense of their nation's position in the world at large, a far more multitudinous, fragmented, and disagreeable world in which, as Pliny once remarked, there were more gods than people.[45]

In reality, though, Rabbinic society, far from being so harmonious and unified, was often rent by dissension and by acrimonious, prolonged disputes among sages. Many individual Rabbis led schools with their private disciples. Moreover, the collective body of sages in each generation appears to have composed a fiercely argumentative and independent class that sometimes opposed the decisions of the patriarch, the officially recognized leader of the Palestinian Jewish community and the head of the main Rabbinic court. As we saw in the story about Rabbi Eliezer ben Hyrkanus, such episodes of contention between individual sages and the patriarch were not infrequent.[46] Especially during the first hundred years following the destruction of the Temple in 70 C.E., the major task faced by the patriarch—first Gamliel II, later his son Simon ben Gamliel—was to consolidate Palestinian Jewry under the form of the specific religious vision that eventually came to be known as Rabbinic Judaism. This task required the patriarch to unify a highly fragmented society as well as a corpus of diverse beliefs and practices. The task of unification was not accomplished easily; indeed, the endemic divisiveness that was a source of tragic factionalism in Palestinian Judaism as well as a source of its individualism and creativity was never entirely eradicated. The patriarchs themselves at times were arrogant and authoritarian, and their behavior exacerbated already tense situations. Precisely how strife-ridden the internal political situation of Rabbinic Judaism actually was can be gauged by the fact that both Gamliel and his son Simon faced attempts by other sages to depose them from their hereditary offices. The story of the deposition of Rabban Gamliel is one of the better-known incidents in Rabbinic history.

That story is also directly relevant to the larger Talmudic passage in Hagigah from which the lengthy sermon of Rabbi Eleazar quoted earlier was taken; in fact, if it is read against the backdrop of the story of Gamliel's deposition, Rabbi Eleazar's sermon also takes on a somewhat different meaning. In concluding this chapter, I want to explore this other reading and its implications for our larger concerns about the relationship between midrash and literary theory.

As the Talmud presents it, the attempted deposition followed upon a series of three confrontations between the patriarch Gamliel and one of the more distinguished sages of the generation, Joshua ben Hananiah.[47] In each confrontation, Joshua dared to teach halakhic rulings opposed to the patriarch's; Gamliel responded to what he considered Joshua's insubordination by publicly humiliating him. The other sages, outraged by the patriarch's behavior, voted to depose Gamliel and to appoint another sage, Rabbi Eleazar ben Azariah, to the patriarchate.

After being deposed, however, Gamliel was persuaded to apologize to Joshua, and when the latter accepted his apology, Gamliel was allowed to reassume his former position. At the same time, the sages, in deference to Rabbi Eleazar, created a new office for him, president of the high court, and also granted Eleazar the privilege of preaching the Sabbath sermon in the academy at Yavneh every third week. That Sabbath became known as "the Sabbath of Rabbi Eleazar."

The confrontation between Gamliel and Joshua probably took place around the years 100–110 C.E. Sometime after Gamliel was reinstated as patriarch, the event narrated in the following passage in Hagigah (B. Hagigah 3a–b) is supposed to have taken place:

> Once Rabbi Yohanan ben Beroka and Rabbi Eleazar Hisma went to pay their respects to Rabbi Joshua [ben Hananiah] at Pekiin. [Rabbi Joshua] asked them: What new teaching was there at the house of study today? They replied: We are your disciples, and we drink your waters. He said to them: Even so, it is impossible for a study session to pass without some new teaching. Whose Sabbath was it? [They answered:] It was the Sabbath of Rabbi Eleazar ben Azariah. [He asked:] So what was the theme of his sermon today? They responded: The biblical section that begins, "Assemble" (Deut. 31:10–13). [Rabbi Joshua asked:] And how did he interpret it? [They replied:] [Scripture says,] "Assemble the people, the men and the women and the children." If the men came to learn and the women came to listen, why did children have to come? In order to reward those that brought them. [Rabbi Joshua] said to them: That was a precious gem you held in your hands, and you wished to deprive me of it?! [His students continued: Rabbi Eleazar] also expounded: "You have affirmed this day that the Lord is your God . . . and the Lord has affirmed this day that you are His treasured people" (Deut. 26:17–18). The Holy One, blessed be He, said to Israel: You have made me a unique object of your love in the world, and I shall make you a unique object of My love in the world. You have made me a unique object of your love, as it is written, "Hear O Israel, the Lord our God, the Lord is One" (Deut. 6:4). And I will make you a unique object of My love, as it is said, "And who is like Your people Israel, a unique nation on earth . . . ?" (1 Chron. 17:21).
>
> [At this point the sermon on Eccles. 12:11, quoted earlier, is cited.]
>
> [Rabbi Joshua then] said to [his two disciples]: The generation in which Rabbi Eleazar ben Azariah lives is not an orphan.

Rabbis Yohanan ben Beroka and Eleazar Hisma were two disciples of Rabbi Joshua ben Hananiah. On their way home from the central academy at Yavneh, they stopped at Pekiin to pay respects to their teacher, who was living, it seems from the narrative, in some isolation from the other sages. When he asked his students what they had learned in the main academy, they replied, "We are your disciples, and we drink your waters." This answer can be read at least two ways. According to traditional commentators, the disciples' response expresses their humility in their teacher's presence. We are your students, they tell him. You teach us; we do not presume to instruct you.[48] The same statement, however, can be understood not as showing the students' dutiful respect to their teacher but as party loyalty. We are your students, they tell Joshua, and we do not study with other teachers—a sentiment that would reflect the factionalism of the Yavneh generation. If that is the meaning of their statement, Rabbi Joshua's response to them is a rebuke: *Still,* you must have learned something at the academy. He then asks whose Sabbath it was, and their reply, "the Sabbath of Rabbi Eleazar ben Azariah," immediately recalls the controversy over the patriarch Gamliel's authoritarian behavior, his abuse of Rabbi Joshua, *our* Rabbi Joshua, now living in Pekiin at a distance from the main academy in Yavneh, whose intellectual exchange he clearly seems to miss, at least enough to want to hear from his disciples what his fellow sages are teaching.

Chastened by their teacher's rebuke, Rabbis Yohanan and Eleazar proceed to rehearse for Rabbi Joshua the three homilies they heard at the academy. At the outset it should be stated that the collocation of these separate homilies in a single literary context is almost certainly an invention of the Talmud's editor. It is highly unlikely that Rabbi Eleazar actually delivered all three homilies on a single occasion; moreover, the individual sermons are found separately elsewhere in Rabbinic literature, a fact that probably attests to their original independence from one another.[49] Nonetheless, all three homilies raise issues that are relevant, more or less directly, to the frame story and its background in the conflict between Gamliel and Joshua.

The first of these homilies comments on Deut. 31:10–13, a passage in which Moses commands the priests to read the law before the entire nation on the holiday of Tabernacles every eighth year. The fulfillment of this command was later assumed by the king of Israel, an important fact since the patriarchal family claimed direct descent from the royal House of David. On the one hand, the substance of the homily stresses the unity of the Israelite community and its shared activity of study, thereby recalling the social fantasy that the concept of polysemy implies, as we have seen. On the other hand, it is difficult to read the homily without remembering the story of Eleazar's appointment to the patriarchate following Gamliel's deposition, the political conflicts behind that appointment, and all the social ramifications of that incident. For Rabbi Eleazar, on "his" Sabbath, to preach a sermon on a biblical text that itself might serve as an archetype for all subsequent patriarchal sermons might almost be construed as a claim to the patriarchal throne. The entire homily, then, may have a politically incendiary message.

The second small homily, in contrast, speaks of the relationship between God and Israel, the uniqueness of each party in the other's estimation, and, perhaps most important, Israel's difference from all other nations in God's eyes. This homily returns us to the Rabbis' need to affirm their identity as God's elect nation, an affirmation that for the Rabbis was directly connected to the activity of midrash and its ideology of interpretation.[50]

The third homily, as we have seen, presents an idealized picture of interpretive pluralism.[51] Yet the very idealism of that picture, the happy coexistence of opposites envisioned within its fantasy, is undercut by the troubling ambiguity of the very conclusion of the passage, that is, Rabbi Joshua's final statement to his disciples. As ostensible praise of his colleague, Joshua's declaration—"The generation in which Rabbi Eleazar ben Azariah lives is not an orphan"—appears by virtue of its negative form to suggest the very opposite of what it states: to imply, in other words, that his, Joshua's, generation is indeed orphaned, that it lacks a leader or proper leadership, that it is defenseless as an orphan, equally protectorless, and likely to be oppressed and victimized. That sentiment returns us again to the unhappy factionalism of early Rabbinic Judaism. It also echoes another statement Rabbi Joshua is reputed once to have made, "Woe to the generation of which you are the leader!" This was the rhetorical lament he addressed to Gamliel when the deposed patriarch came to him to apologize.[52]

In its entirety, then, this passage presents two nearly contradictory impressions. The first of these, common to all the homilies but epitomized in the lengthy third homily we analyzed in detail, conveys a nearly utopian vision of Rabbinic society, a fantasy of harmonious opposition where conflict is literally fruitful, and in which the words of Torah grow like plants and lead from death to life even if they are also goads and sharp as nails. In this fantasy, difference exists (as surely as do the differences among men, women, and children), but the resolution of such difference is seen as an essentially benign process. Difference is ultimately overcome and transcended through the shared participation of all Israelites in Torah study, in the relationship of divine election that Israel's occupation in Torah study signifies. In contrast to this portrait of benign conflict resolution, however, the frame for the homilies, the narrative context for their recitation, alludes to a very different evaluation of conflict and its adjudication, even over "matters of Torah." This evaluation sees conflict as a malignant presence and its resolution as the violent exercise of power, as indeed it sometimes was in Rabbinic society.

The events to which the narrative frame alludes, though they may not be entirely factual historically, represent what Edward Said has called the "worldly" aspects of the text, the human and social conditions out of which the homilies in the passage came into being.[53] Yet these aspects, with their unhappy implications about the nature of social reality, tend to undermine the idealized portrait of interpretive pluralism portrayed in the homilies. The homilies, in turn, when viewed from the perspective of the frame, appear almost as a kind of rhetorical denial of historical reality, a reality that persists in making its presence felt within the text even as it is being denied.

Admittedly, such a reading of the text is nascently deconstructive. Yet it provides us with a peculiarly bound and limited meaning for this text about polysemy: it posits a historical condition and presents the passage as a formation, albeit a negative one, of that condition. What would the Rabbis themselves have made of this reading? It surely would not have been acceptable to them, but not, I would propose, on account of its skepticism, its cynical suspicions about their ideology and about the fantasies that may have motivated that ideology. Rather, I believe that the Rabbis would have acknowledged that the concept of polysemy was a formation or product of something else. They would have located that effective cause not in their historical situation but in the act of Scriptural exegesis itself, that is to say, in the very midrash of Eccles. 12:11 that Rabbi Eleazar presented in his homily. They would have said, in other words, that divine Scripture, if read correctly, dictates its own polysemous reading.

Now this view, the Rabbis' reading, may itself be contextualized and explained historically, but for a theoretical reading of the passage, for understanding the relationship between midrash and theory, it has other implications. The most significant of these is that Scriptural exegesis, midrash, is not identical with literary theory or simply reducible to it. What a theoretical reading of midrash can contribute is precisely an understanding of the difference between midrash and theory, between (for one thing) the role midrash played for the Rabbis, which was to maintain the presence of Scripture (and thereby of God) in their lives, and the function that theory fulfills, which is to strengthen our acts of reading and to deepen (sometimes by undermining) our understanding of them. The difference separating these conceptions is at least one sign of the distance that interpretation has traveled in the course of history.

Chapter 2

Forms of Midrash I: Parables of Interpretation

For many students of literature, the idea of midrash may most immediately suggest the ways in which one text and its meaning are to be found in another, that is, the very exegetical features buried within works of fiction and poetry. In the study of midrash itself, however, the nature of its "literariness" becomes an issue not at the point where literature becomes exegesis but where exegesis turns into literature, where it comes to possess its own language and voice. In the previous chapter, I discussed the problematic connection between the hermeneutics of midrash and literary theory. In this chapter and in chapter 3, I wish to discuss midrash as literary discourse in its own right.

As we shall see, the literary forms of midrash are not irrelevant to its hermeneutics. Yet to understand these forms, the first duty of a literary approach to midrash, as paradoxical as it may seem, must be to suspend temporarily our more immediate concerns with "literature"—that is, our preconceptions as to what constitutes literature and what we are accustomed to consider its formal properties—and to go over, as it were, to the other side in order to describe the specific language of midrash and the special conditions that created its singular literary forms and modes of expression. This is necessary whether those forms and modes are the recognizable techniques of narrative or whether they constitute the more unusual exegetical vehicles that are often far more typical of midrashic discourse.

In this chapter, I want to discuss perhaps the most clearly definable form of narrative in midrash, the parable or *mashal*. Yet as soon as the student of midrash embarks upon the project of defining a literary form in midrash, he or she encounters what is probably the most frustrating feature of Rabbinic literature in general, namely, its reticence—how little it reveals of the story of its own making, about the situations and circumstances in which its texts originated, let alone about its more "theoretical" underpinnings. A partial exception to this general rule may be the following rather amusing narrative from Vayikra Rabbah:

> Shimeon, the son of Rabbi [Judah], prepared a [wedding] banquet for his son. He went and invited all the sages, but he forgot to invite Bar Kappara.

[Bar Kappara] went and wrote on the door [of Rabbi Shimeon's house]: After rejoicing is death. So what value is there to rejoicing? Rabbi Shimeon asked: Who did this to me? Is there anyone we did not invite?

Someone said: Bar Kappara. You forgot to invite him. Rabbi Shimeon remarked: To invite [Bar Kappara] now by himself would be unseemly.

So [Rabbi Shimeon] went and made a second banquet, and he invited all the sages, and he also invited Bar Kappara. But at every course that was brought in to the guests, Bar Kappara recited three hundred fox fables. The guests did not even taste the dishes before they grew cold, and the dishes were removed from the table just as they had been brought in. Rabbi Shimeon asked his servant: Why are all the dishes being returned untouched?

[The servant] replied: Because there is an old man sitting there, and at every course he tells fables until the dishes grow cold, and no one eats them.

Rabbi Shimeon went up to [Bar Kappara] and said: What have I done to make you ruin my banquet?

Bar Kappara responded: Do I need your banquet? Did not Solomon say, "What real value is there for a man in all the gains he makes beneath the sun?" (Eccles. 1:3) And what is written after that verse? "One generation goes, another comes, but the earth remains the same forever" (Eccles. 1:4).[1]

Unhappily, this passage tells us nothing about the three hundred fox fables—*matlin* or *meshalim*—that Bar Kappara recited over every course at Rabbi Shimeon's banquet. In fact, the passage doesn't bother to record even a single mashal, possibly because the fables, entertaining as they must have been, were not considered sufficiently "serious" to be preserved in writing.[2] Even so, the passage is revealing, if only for what it suggests about the nature of the mashal as a literary form and its function as an allusive narrative with an unspoken message. In Bar Kappara's case, the very act of reciting the mashal served an ulterior purpose. It offered him a clever if somewhat nasty means to retaliate against his host for the insult he felt he had earlier suffered.[3]

Admittedly, revenge is an unusual motive for parable-making. Elsewhere in Rabbinic literature, other motives, purposes, and occasions for the mashal are depicted. Some sages are reported to have used the mashal as an oblique means of expressing political opinions that were too dangerous to be stated openly.[4] Other sages are said to have employed the literary form as an effective weapon for responding to polemical attacks by outsiders (very much the way Jesus is portrayed in the Gospels as fashioning parables to argue with the Jewish leaders who oppose him).[5] Still other sages used the parable as a tactful instrument for smoothing over socially awkward or embarrassing situations as well as for praising the dead, either in eulogies or in the course of consoling grieving relatives.[6] Several sources preserve meshalim of this type. One text relates how Rabbi Yohanan ben Zakkai recited two meshalim about himself even as he lay in bed dying![7]

The most frequent occasion for use of the mashal, however, was the sermon in the synagogue or the lecture in the Rabbinic academy. Surprisingly, there exist no literary descriptions of meshalim delivered in these institutional contexts.[8] Still, it seems highly probable that most of the approximately one thousand meshalim recorded in Rabbinic literature were at least intended to be used in these institutions as material for sermons or lessons.[9] It is therefore only appropriate that the most common literary context in which meshalim are preserved in Rabbinic literature is that of midrash. It was midrash that determined the conventional two-part structure of the mashal, consisting of a narrative (the mashal proper) and a *nimshal*, the so-called explanation or (as I prefer to call it) application of the narrative. And it was midrash, too, that gave the Rabbinic mashal its explicit raison d'être, which was to be an exegetical tool, a device for interpreting Scripture and for arriving at its meaning.

The Rabbis themselves believed that the mashal was invented (according to one tradition, by King Solomon) in order to reveal the secrets of Torah.[10] To make this very point, the Rabbis recited a mashal *about* the mashal:

> It is like a king who lost a gold piece in his house, or a valuable gem. Does he not find it by means of a penny candle?
>
> Likewise: Let not the mashal seem trivial in your eyes, for by means of the mashal a man is able to understand the words of Torah.[11]

What is trivial about the mashal is its fictionality, a fictionality legitimated or "saved," as it were, by the exegetical instrumentality of the mashal. Now we need not accept the Rabbis' estimation of the mashal's value (worth no more than a penny candle) in order to appreciate their view that the mashal is a didactic literary form, a story with a message. But the real object of that message is not exegesis per se; it is an ideology, a worldview—specifically, the ideology of Rabbinic Judaism. The mashal is an ideological narrative, and the Rabbis used it, as they used Sciptural exegesis, to impress upon their audience the validity and authority of their view of the world.[12] And the reason why Scriptural exegesis, midrash, was so effective a tool for ideological communication of this kind was because the Rabbis were fully persuaded that the Torah expressed their vision of Judaism as God's will for the world.

Form, as we know, follows function. And we have just seen the many functions that the mashal served for the Rabbis. But form is not identical with function, and it was the form of the mashal that proved so attractive to the Rabbis. What was that form? How did it arise? How could it be so adaptable, so able to serve the Rabbis in so many different contexts and on so many occasions?

We can begin to answer these questions by saying that there is no single explanation or model that will explain comprehensively the traits of all meshalim in Rabbinic literature (let alone all parables in world literature). In fact, there are at least three separate models for conceptualizing the mashal, and these three models lie along a kind of spectrum of parabolic possibilities. Two of the three form the extremities of the spectrum: at one end, the parable as an illustrative or demonstrational narrative; at the other, as a mode of secret or concealing speech. Between these two poles lies a third model, the mashal as a rhetorical narrative. In my view, most Rabbinic meshalim may be grouped under this last model, that is, somewhere between the two extreme poles of open illustration and secret speech. Nonetheless, certain Rabbinic meshalim are closer in character to one of the other two models; and in the course of the mashal's history in Hebrew literature, from the Bible until Agnon (nearly), the parable has been used at different times in conformity with all three models. Each one, accordingly, warrants a brief description before we proceed to our main subject, the Rabbinic mashal.

The Mashal as Illustration

In this view, the mashal is a medium for illustrating abstract ideas or beliefs through narrative examples that are concrete, familiar, and thus (this is the primary assumption behind this model) more easily comprehended by an audience that is believed to be inherently incapable of grasping such abstractions on its own and therefore requires the "help" of the parable. In this conceptualization, highly influential in New Testament parable scholarship since the nineteenth century, the mashal is a kind of simile, an explicit figure for likeness and resemblance.[13]

The application of this model to the Rabbinic mashal is a complicated matter.[14] There are certainly many instances in Talmudic and midrashic texts where the mashal is used as an illustration. In Bereshit Rabbah 1:15, two oft-quoted meshalim, attributed to the Houses of Hillel and Shammai, appear as responses to the question of what was created first in the universe—the heavens (according to the House of Shammai) or the earth (according to the House of Hillel).

> According to the House of Shammai, it is like a king who built a throne for himself, and then made a footstool to go with it, as it is written, ". . . The heaven is My throne and the earth is My footstool" (Isa. 66:1).
>
> According to the House of Hillel, it is like a king who built a palace; after he built the ground floor, he built the upper stories, as it is written, ". . . on the day when the Lord made earth and heaven" (Gen. 2:4).

As illustrations, these two examples seem at first glance to be wholly straightforward. Yet they do considerably more than merely illustrate the two houses' respective views of the order of creation. Each mashal's narrative also predicates a different conception of the nature of the created universe and of God's relationship to it. According to one house, the earth is God's footstool; according to the other, it is His palace.

In literature from the Rabbinic period, one can find other parables of this illustrational kind.[15] But it is not until post-Rabbinic, early medieval Jewish times that the use of the mashal as an illustration becomes the prevalent form. It occurs initially in the ninth-century composition *Tanna de-Bei Eliyahu,* and becomes even more prevalent in subsequent philosophical works by such authors as Maimonides.[16] For the vast majority of meshalim in Rabbinic literature, however, the illustrational model does not offer an adequate description. Most midrashic meshalim are far less illustrative than the examples above. Even more crucially, the narratives of most meshalim, which this model asserts are supposed to facilitate and assist their audience in understanding the mashal's lesson or its underlying meaning, are actually far more enigmatic and difficult to understand than the nimshalim themselves. In these parables, what requires elucidation is the narrative, not the nimshal or its lesson. Considered as illustrations, these meshalim are horrible failures.

The Mashal as Secret Speech

This model, the near opposite of the preceding one, conceives of the mashal as a deliberately occluding and concealing mode of language. As such, it resembles the view that identifies the mashal with allegory (which is, indeed, what the word *mashal* comes to mean as a technical term in medieval Hebrew). The "allegorical" view itself is first expressed in the Gospels, in the famous theory of parabolic discourse attributed to Jesus (Mark 4:11–12 and parallels), while among modern scholars it has been most elegantly championed by Frank Kermode, who sees *all* narrative as enigmatic and excluding, having the "property of banishing interpreters from its secret places."[17] For Kermode, the parable is merely a purer, more intense or pristine instance of this general characteristic of narrative.

According to this model, the mashal is an intrinsically esoteric form. It is an interpretive shield guarding a secret meaning, separating "insiders" from "outsiders" and restricting access to comprehension to a select, chosen few.[18] In a corollary often associated with this model of the mashal, the literary form is typically used in politically or religiously oppresive situations in order to express controversial or dangerous beliefs that one could not articulate openly, either for political or doctrinal reasons.[19]

The Rabbis themselves would probably have appreciated this conception of the mashal. For example, they interpret Yotham's seditious parable in Judges 9:7–20 as an allegory.[20] And a few other passages in Rabbinic literature corroborate the "secretive" use of the parable. The best example of these is the statement in Bereshit Rabbah 22:19, attributed to Rabbi Shimeon ben Yohai: "It is difficult really to express it, and impossible to explain." This statement prefaces a mashal that in effect condemns God for letting Cain kill Abel. But this mashal and the few others like it are truly exceptions in Rabbinic literature.[21] As a mode of secretive, exclusive discourse, the mashal does not emerge in its full shape until the beginning of kabbalistic literature in the early Middle Ages, first in the many enigmatic meshalim preserved in *Sefer Hababir* and later in the elegant parables found in the Zohar.[22] Within Rabbinic tradition, the communicational model for the mashal is exoteric, not esoteric. Even where a mashal's message is ambiguous or especially subtle and difficult to paraphrase, that message can be "interpreted out" of the mashal by any minimally competent reader.

The Mashal as Rhetorical Narrative

This model steers a course between the two poles represented in the preceding models. In my view, it is the model that accounts for *most* meshalim in Rabbinic literature. Here the mashal is an allusive narrative told for an ulterior purpose: it draws a series of parallels between a fictional story and the actual, "real-life" situation to which the mashal is directed.[23] Rather than make those parallels explicit, however, the mashal leaves them to its audience to figure out. This is the inherently hermeneutic character of the form, and no doubt a major reason why the mashal was so popular among the Rabbis. Neither a secret tale with a hidden meaning nor a transparent story with a clear-cut moral, the mashal is a narrative that actively elicits from its audience the application of its message—or what we would call its interpretation.

Consider the following mashal from Vayikra Rabbah 2:4, whose author, Rabbi Berechiah, was a fourth-century Palestinian sage.

> Rabbi Berechiah said: It is like an elder who had a robe [*ma'aforet*]. He commanded his disciple, saying: Fold it and iron it and be very careful.
>
> The disciple asked: My master, O elder! Of all the robes you own, why do you command me only about this one?
>
> The elder replied: Because that robe is the one I wore the day I was appointed an elder!
>
> Likewise: Moses said before the Holy One: Master of the Universe! Of all seventy self-ruling nations that you have in the world, you command me only regarding Israel?!

He replied: For they accepted my sovereignty at Mount Sinai and declared, "All that the Lord has spoken we will do and we will obey" (Exod. 24:7).

The exegetical occasion for this mashal, its prooftext, is Exod. 24:7, which here is understood to be a literal acknowledgment on the part of the people of Israel of *kabalat 'ol malkhut shamayim,* the acceptance of God's sovereignty. The mashal's principal message, however, is not praise of God but of Israel, and that praise is expressed in terms of Israel's uniqueness in God's eyes. Yet this unique status derives, in turn, from the praise, the *doxa,* the special glory, that Israel paid to God—a theme that is raised by the central image in the mashal's narrative, the image of the robe. This image, as Saul Lieberman has pointed out, refers to the *ma'aforet,* the special ceremonial robe of office that an elder sage assumed upon appointment.[24] As it is employed in the mashal, the image is also a rather bold one, for it suggests that God, too, was not "appointed" to his office until the children of Israel elected Him at Mount Sinai—a fairly radical theological idea that appears elsewhere in Rabbinic literature.[25] This idea only intensifies the high praise paid to Israel.

The same message of praise informs the exegesis of Exod. 24:7, the mashal's prooftext, which culminates the nimshal or application of the narrative (the second part of the normative literary form, which begins, in the example above, with the word "likewise"). The full "parabolic" meaning of that exegesis might be paraphrased as follows: Even though the Jews, unlike the seventy Gentile nations, do not have an independent or self-ruling political state of their own (a fact that doubtless emphasized a pointed and sad truth for Jews living in Palestine in the fourth century), they are still dearer to God than all the Gentile nations because Israel alone accepted God's sovereignty, His law, at Sinai.

Praise of Israel is therefore achieved indirectly here through a comparison with the other nations. To that extent, this mashal involves a degree of polemic, and if we had to describe its message or theme in a single phrase, we could call it polemicized praise.[26] Most meshalim in Rabbinic literature have a comparable rhetorical function. They express thematic messages, but those messages tend to be *phrased* in terms of either praise or blame, or a variant of the two: approbation or disapproval, appreciation or disappointment, pleasure or pain. While praise and blame are not in themselves the mashal's meaning, they are its structures of signification, the critical terms in its rhetorical vocabulary. Through praise and blame, the mashal communicates its thematic and ideological messages. These messages, though in theory numberless, can in practice be specified rather easily: apologetics; polemics; consolation (often formulated as eulogy, praise of the dead); complaint (blame directed against the mashal's addressee, a character usually figuring in the mashal's own narrative, for the unfairness of his behavior); regret (in which the mashal's protagonist reconsiders his or her act of praise or blame);

warning (in which the mashal anticipates, as it were, its act of blame or praise); and a few others.[27]

In the remainder of this chapter, I wish to analyze in detail one mashal that, as we shall see, explicitly communicates one message of praise and simultaneously hints at a second message closer to blame. The mashal is found in Eikhah Rabbah, the classical midrash on the book of Lamentations, as well as in several other sources. Its author, Rabbi Abba bar Kahana, was another fourth-century Palestinian sage. I will first quote the mashal's narrative, its mashal proper.[28]

> Rabbi Abba bar Kahana said: It is like a king who married a woman and wrote her a large dowry [*ketubah*]. He wrote to her: So many bridal chambers I make for you; so much jewelry I make for you; so much gold and silver I give you. Then he left her for many years and journeyed to the provinces. Her neighbors used to taunt her and say: Hasn't your husband abandoned you? Go! Marry another man.
>
> She would weep and sigh, and afterward, she would enter her bridal chamber and read her marriage settlement and console herself. Many years and days later the king returned. He said to her: I am amazed that you have waited for me all these years!
>
> She replied: My master, O king! If not for the large dowry you wrote me, my neighbors would have led me astray long ago.

The mashal's symbolism is nearly all conventional and does not require elaborate explanation: the king represents God, his consort the people of Israel, the dowry or *ketubah* the Torah.[29] Even so, it is important that we not miss the sometimes remarkable use to which these symbols, despite their conventionality, are put in the mashal. Consider the helpless consort, a stock figure in some respects but a very unusual character in others. As Kathryn Hellerstein has reminded me, how many other texts in Rabbinic literature—or in ancient literature in general—depict a woman who literally survives through reading, or who reads to survive? Or consider the taunts of the neighbors, words that at first glance might appear to be the typical provocations that wicked neighbors would be expected to use in order to arouse the insecurities and fears of a lonely, vulnerable woman. But, in fact, this motif may be the mashal's most historically grounded detail. According to Roman law, marriage must be by consent, *maritalis affectio,* namely, "the intention to be in the married state." In regard to such intention, the second-century jurist Ulpian specifically discusses cases where husband and wife have lived apart for a long time—exactly as in our mashal—and states that if each one has honored the marriage, they are still married, "for it is not cohabitation which makes a marriage but *maritalis affectio*."[30] The neighbors in our mashal, however, may be said to raise precisely the opposite possibility: since the king disappeared so suddenly, perhaps he *has* abandoned his wife and has *not* been faithful to her. If so, she, the consort, is indeed no longer bound to him in marriage. According to the law, she is actually free to marry another man, as the neighbors encourage her to do. She, of course, refuses this "interpretation" of her husband's absence. Nonetheless, in the mashal's own historical context within the Greco-Roman world, the neighbors' "interpretation" may have been the more plausible one; it was certainly not completely improbable or purely malicious.

Such historically grounded detail is crucial for understanding the mashal's rhetoric. The rhetorical mode of this mashal is clearly praise. In fact, it is doubled praise. At first, the king praises his wife for remaining faithful to him during the long period of his absence; in response, the consort offers her own praise of the ketubah, which, she says, gave her the strength to await her husband's return despite her unhappy, isolated situation. That situation is elaborated more fully in the nimshal:

> Likewise: The nations of the world taunt Israel and say to them: Your God does not want you. He has left you. He has removed His presence from you. Come with us. We will appoint you to be generals, governors, and officers.
>
> And the people of Israel enter their synagogues and houses of study, and there they read in the Torah, "I will look with favor upon you, and make you fertile. . . . I will establish My abode in your midst, and I will not spurn you" (Lev. 26:9, 11), and they console themselves.
>
> In the future, when the redemption comes, the Holy One, blessed be He, says to Israel: My children! I am amazed at how you have waited for Me all these years.
>
> And they say to Him: Master of the Universe! Were it not for the Torah you gave us, in which we read when we entered our synagogues and houses of study, "I will look with favor upon you . . . and I will not spurn you," the nations of the world would have led us astray long ago.
>
> That is what is written, "Were not your teaching my delight, I would have perished in my affliction" (Ps. 119:92). Therefore it says, "This [*zot*] I call to mind; therefore I have hope" (Lam. 3:21).

Our analysis of the mashal will begin with its conclusion, the exegesis of Lam. 3:21. In its Scriptural context, this verse is spoken by the *gever,* the unnamed male who is both the protagonist of the chapter and its speaker. In the preceding twenty verses, the gever has despairingly described how he has been cruelly hunted down and tortured by an all-powerful antagonist, whom *we* know to be God but whom the gever cannot bring himself to name. In verse 21, however, that of the mashal, there is a sudden shift in the gever's lament. For no apparent reason, without any obvious motivation, he remembers "this," *zot,* and from that moment on he begins to recover his confidence and regain hope.

Now in Lamentations itself, "this"—what the gever recalls—is a series of discursive propositions that are spelled out in the subsequent verses. These propositions all concern God's nature—His essential goodness, how His mercies are never spent, how ample is His grace, how good He is to those who trust in Him, and so on. In the mashal, however, the word *zot,* "this," is interpreted so as to refer not to God but to Torah—specifically to the Torah's promises of redemption, as symbolized in the narrative by the image of the ketubah and its promised bridal gifts. To be sure, this interpretation recalls the famous midrash on Deut. 4:44, *vezot hatorah,* "and this is the Torah," which is explicitly quoted in some of the parallel versions of our mashal.[31] Yet it is hard to think of another interpretation that could be more revealing of Rabbinic ideology than this one, with its shifting of meaning from God to the Torah as the referent for the demonstrative *zot.* As Alan Mintz has noted, Lam. 3:21 is the pivotal verse in the chapter, the precise moment when the gever turns from despair to faith.[32] At precisely this moment, Rabbi Abba's interpretation, with its substitution of Torah for God, virtually sums up the achievement of Rabbinic Judaism in instituting Torah study as the practical and theoretical foundation for Israel's spiritual sustenance in the time of exile, as the replacement for the lost Temple cult, and as the medium of access to the divine will in the aftermath of the destruction of the Temple.

The exegesis of *zot* in Lam. 3:21 is only one of several exegetical acts in the mashal. In fact, this mashal in praise of Torah and its study—in praise of midrash, in other words—is fittingly packed with midrash and with the products of midrash, including references to other midrashim and allusions to extrabiblical aggadot. For example, the taunting words that the nations of the world address to Israel in the nimshal allude to the famous midrash on Song of Songs 5:9–6:3, found both in the *Mekhilta* (Shirta 3, where it is attributed to Rabbi Akiba) and in *Sifre Deuteronomy* 343. Similarly, the verses from Leviticus (Lev. 26:9, 11) cited in the nimshal have a lengthy history of interpretation, which can be traced all the way back to the Tannaitic collection *Sifra* (Behukotai 1:2.5, 1:3.3); there the Rabbis interpreted the verses eschatologically, as blessings to be fulfilled only at the time of the final redemption. Since these verses are invoked in the nimshal to comfort the people of Israel, we can assume that Rabbi Abba also intended his audience to understand them as referring to the future redemption (otherwise the disparity between the dire reality and the promises of the verse would be anything but comforting). As they are cited in the nimshal, then, these verses are quoted in their *already-interpreted* sense.

Moreover, the mashal's central image, the ketubah, may itself be an exegetical creation. It is possible that the image derives from a pun on the Hebrew word *vehifreiti,* "I will make you fruitful," in Lev. 26:9, and the Aramaic *parna,* borrowed from the Greek *pherne,* a marriage settlement.[33] This punning etymology would provide a reason why these particular verses from Leviticus were chosen for the nimshal, and it would explain why the ketubah is so prominent an image in the mashal. Thus the mashal may be said to contain within its narrative the key to its own beginnings as a midrashic act.

Exegesis, though, is not the final intention or whole purpose of the mashal. If the verses from Leviticus are to be read eschatologically, as I have suggested, then the narrative in its entirety takes on a new meaning. When the king returns to his wife after his lengthy absence, he may be said, *in narrative terms,* to fulfill and realize the promises of Scripture. In other words, the mashal's narrative can be seen as dramatizing the coming redemption before its audience's eyes; the narrative reenacts the Scriptural promises. The consolation the consort is seen to have derived from reading her ketubah is thus guaranteed to the mashal's contemporary audience. And so the mashal ceases to be simply a parable of praise and becomes a narrative of consolation. But why should that consolation be necessary in the first place? Why, we might ask, must the poor *matrona* suffer? Why does the king abandon her? Why must she be left alone, subject to her neighbors' persecutions and torments? If her ordeal is a test of faithfulness, why must she submit to such a test when she has done nothing to deserve it?

These questions raise issues that are both theological and historical, and that could be answered accordingly. For our present purposes, however, it will be more appropriate to frame them in narratalogical terms. We might ask further: Why does the king suddenly decide to journey to the foreign provinces? Does it ever enter the king's mind that in his absence the wicked neighbors will torment his wife and test her? Are the lavish promises he makes in the ketubah intended *in advance* to console her while he is gone? Are his promises sincere? If they are, then why is he so astonished at her faithfulness? Conversely, if he does not expect the ketubah to console his bereft wife, then is there any logical reason for her to remain faithful? Or are his promises disingenuous? Is the king's unexplained absence truly unjustified? Is he perhaps guilty of gratuitous cruelty toward his hapless wife? Is he actually responsible in his own person for the suffering his abandoned wife undergoes in his absence? And why does he finally decide to return?

I have posed these questions not to answer them but to show how the various doubts contained in them are inevitably raised by the mashal's narrative. These doubts point in the direction of a critique of the king's behavior and of the justice of his actions—which is to say, toward a critical interrogation of God and His treatment of Israel. This critique, though never quite explicit in the mashal, undercuts the innocent optimism of our earlier "rhetorical" reading of the composition as a praise parable and leads to a second reading of the mashal, one closer to complaint than to consolation.

This second reading is connected to another anomalous moment in the text, a small but significant discrepancy between the mashal and the nimshal at a point where their carefully drawn parallels diverge. The mashal's narrative, it will be recalled, is related entirely in the past tense: the king journeyed, he returned, he and his wife were happily reunited. At the point in the nimshal corresponding to the king's return, however, there is a sudden and unanticipated leap into the future that is signaled by one word, *lemahar*. "*In the future*," we are told, "when the redemption comes, the Holy One, blessed be He, says to Israel," and so on.[34] For the mashal's audience, this discontinuity can lead only to a single conclusion: Genuine consolation, the true fulfillment of the promises in Scripture, will come only at the time of redemption, at the end of history. The return of the king in the mashal's narrative was made possible only because fictional narrative, by convention, is narrated in the past tense. But in the realm of historical reality, and as long as that reality—human history—exists, redemption will always be in the future. Until it comes to pass, substitutes alone exist for authentic redemption. Among these substitutes, the foremost, of course, is the study of Torah, midrash. Yet even the study of Torah is not true redemption. It is only a surrogate, a palliative, a Band-Aid covering the wound of history.

In its totality, then, this mashal suggests two very different attitudes or meanings; taken together, they produce a message that is necessarily ambiguous, at least on the interpretive level. To students of literature, the hermeneutical dilemma posed by this ambiguity may recall other famous cases of literary ambiguity—Henry James's *Turn of the Screw*, for example. And, as in James's novella, the "solution" to the hermeneutical conundrum lies not in deciding on a univocal reading—either the explicit consolatory reading or the implied critique—but in reading both messages simultaneously despite the apparent contradiction between them.

The source of that contradiction and its consequent ambiguity can be explored further. For one thing, its real origins may lie not in the king's behavior but in the consort's. For why, after all, does *she* refuse to question her husband's acts, his loyalty, his faithfulness? Does her insistence upon praising the ketubah really indicate a need on her part to deny the truth about her husband's cruelty? Is she perhaps constitutionally incapable of seeing how he has mistreated her? Or does she know something that we, the audience of the mashal, do not?

Again, these are questions that the mashal does not answer, though not, I believe, because they are strategically placed in the narrative to intentionally undercut its accepted meaning or its overt message of praise (as with the set of questions raised above). Rather, these questions actually lie beyond the mashal's own ken, the limits of its own comprehension. They are situated precisely at the farthest end of what we might call the mashal's theological horizon; indeed, they determine its horizon. To appreciate the mashal, its audience must take the consort's faithfulness to the king, like Israel's faithfulness to God, on faith; one cannot question the sincerity of either persona's claim. To be sure, the other ambiguity in the parable—the conflict between complaint and consolation—persists, and if one were to search for its ultimate cause, it might be located in the mashal's author's own mind, in the unresolved nature of his feelings toward God, which may be ambiguous or contradictory. We will return to the question of the Rabbinic-midrashic conception of God in the final chapter. The ambiguity in the consort's mind will not help us to understand the mashal or its author's mind except to fix the one matter, the one question, that he or she would have found literally unthinkable. Indeed, rather than try to dissolve the mashal's inner contradiction or search for a psychological or spiritual explanation, one does better to ask: How can the literary form of the mashal simultaneously communicate two messages so different and yet related to each other? To answer this question, we must turn to the poetics of narrative in the mashal and to its formal features.

The first of these features is its stereotyped, virtually formulaic character. As I have shown elsewhere, nearly every motif in the mashal—its narrative units and themes as well as the diction and phraseology in which those narrative motifs and themes are expressed—is highly conventional.[35] Partly because of this conventional, stereotyped character, narrative representation in the mashal tends toward absolute brevity; in fact, the parabolic narrative is often so concise it is like a skeleton or a sketch rather than a fully fleshed-out tale. Because all but the most necessary details are excluded, everything that *is* said draws the most intense attention. In this conciseness, the mashal's narrative resembles that of the Bible, in which, in Erich Auerbach's famous description, virtually nothing is foregrounded while the entire background is fraught with meaning.[36] Indeed, this point of resemblance may be one of the stronger lines of continuity between the biblical and the Rabbinic literary traditions.

Another characteristic feature of the mashal's narrative poetics is its use of silences, lacunae, omissions, and other such points of discontinuity. Narratologists call these intentionally withheld pieces of narrative information gaps, and each and every one of them can be described systematically.[37] For example, each of the questions raised earlier about Eikhah Rabbah 3:21 relates to a specific type of gap found not only in the mashal but in narrative generally: to missing links in the story; absent causes or motives; failure to offer satisfactory explanations for an occurence in the plot; contradictions (like the discrepancy we noted between the mashal and its nimshal); and, most prominently of all, the discrepancy between its description of God's behavior (as represented in the figure of the king) and our normative conceptions of what God's behavior should be, a gap between expectation and reality.

Reading the gaps in the narrative and "filling" them in by interpreting their significance are the primary hermeneutical activities in which the mashal's audience engages. Indeed, one of the important reasons for the mashal's effectiveness as a narrative form lies in its mastery of the art of gap-creating and gap-filling. In this way, the mashal guides its reader in the right direction, toward filling its gaps and grasping its underlying message. And given the centrality of gaps in the poetics of the mashal, it is not surprising that the activities of reading and interpretation should be imagistically reflected within the mashal itself. Such imagery is perhaps the other most striking feature of the mashal's narrative poetics.

Recent literary theory has familiarized us with the various roles that the reader plays in determining textual meaning. It has also described the different guises through which the figure of the reader can be represented in the fictional structure: the "implied reader," the "narratee," the "interpretant," and the "interpreting character," a figure who (according to one theoretician) is usually "coextensive with the first-person narrator or the main protagonist of the fiction" and through whom "the author is trying to tell the interpreter [the reader] something *about* interpretation."[38]

In the mashal, these various constructions coalesce into a figure I call the implied interpreter: an idealized character in the mashal's narrative who serves as a model for the real interpreter/reader and who guides the latter in the act of reading and interpreting the mashal's meaning. The implied interpreter is not identical with his or her counterpart in real life. To paraphrase Wolfgang Iser on the implied reader, the implied interpreter is a figure *in* the text.[39] The real addressee will always possess certain interpretive resources that he or she will bring to understanding the mashal: knowledge of models of coherence (rules of chronology, causality, etc.); of literary conventions (including the stereotyped character of the mashal's diction, motifs, and themes); of the hermeneutical conventions of midrash (for example: *kal vehomer, notarikon, gematriyah*).[40] But the implied reader is in most ways an ideal interpreter who possesses all the literary competence needed to understand a mashal.[41] As a fictional character, the implied interpreter literally inscribes the relationship of exegesis and narrative in the mashal by joining in his or her single person, or persona, the attributes of both fictionality and interpretation.

To illustrate the implied interpreter's role, we can turn to the meshalim we have already analyzed. In the parable from Vayikra Rabbah about the elder and his robe, the implied interpreter is less an explicit character than a presence to be inferred from an implied interpretive event, or *scene of interpretation,* in the narrative. This scene is sometimes represented in the form of a recognizable hermeneutical operation, like the *kal vehomer,* or through another kind of identifiable interpretive gesture. At other times, an actual scene is created and represented, as in the mashal about the elder. In this case, the elder himself creates a scene of interpretation by commanding his disciple to do something the disciple finds sufficiently extraordinary as to demand an explanation; then the elder himself becomes the implied interpreter with the disciple as his foil, an interpreter's straight man.

In contrast, in Eikhah Rabbah 3:21, the implied interpreter is explicitly represented through the character of the helpless, beleaguered consort who consoles herself by reading the promises her absent husband has left her in the ketubah. This act of reading the ketubah, along with the consort's later explanation (to the king) of its positive effect upon her, is about as complete a representation of the implied interpretive event as can be found in any mashal. Indeed, in this example, the representation of the implied interpreter may exceed the significance of the interpretation itself. After all, Rabbi Abba bar Kahana could have offered his midrash on the word *zot* as meaning Torah without using a mashal; he could have presented it as a definition of the demonstrative simply on the basis of Deut. 4:44 (*vezot hatorah*). What the mashal's narrative really contributes is not so much the exegesis of *zot*, and not even a dramatization of the fulfillment of the eschatological promises of Leviticus, but a vivid and moving portrayal of the conditions of despair in which the poor abandoned wife finds herself. For it is within these conditions that the *necessity* for the eschatological-consolatory interpretation is born. In presenting this picture of despair and consolation, the mashal effectively portrays the history of its own genesis—a narrative of interpretation.

This narrative is not the only narrative of interpretation to be found in midrash, or even in the mashal itself. But it does sketch the basic lineaments of the story. The narrative invariably begins with a crisis, often marked (as here) by a departure or absence, either literal or figurative. The crisis involves the disappearance not of meaning but of presence (the king's, God's), and it is followed by the characters' growing consciousness of the void, the emptiness and irresolution, in which they have been left. If the mashal's narrative can be said to reach a conclusion, the resolution comes through an interpretive event—not one that aims to discover meaning in the text, but one that aims to restore the absent presence, the guarantor of meaning. Its real aim is the restoration of a feeling of intimacy and affinity with the estranged text, and thereby with God. In this narrative, exegesis approaches the radical meaning of interpretation as "a presence between," that is, as a literal mediator or mediating activity. The act of interpretation becomes primarily a medium for exchange while the interpreter functions above all as a translator, literally one who carries the text across a divide, who negotiates the distance between Scripture and its felt presence in the reader's life. As Eikhah Rabbah 3:21 suggests, interpretation itself may not be the promised end, but it is the invaluable preparation that leads to such an end.

As we saw in the previous chapter, it is difficult to specify the precise hermeneutical underpinnings of midrash. Rather than possessing a hermeneutics, a systematic base for interpretation, midrash may be said to have been impelled by a narrative of interpretation. Accordingly, the goal of a theoretical study of midrash would be less a matter of hermeneutics, of learning the system of interpretive procedures, than a project of constructing a narratology.

The narrative of interpretation points to the essential impulse behind the midrashic mashal: the desire to represent in and through narrative the special kind of interpretation that midrash constitutes. Indeed, it is the poetics of that metanarrative that a narratology of the mashal ultimately serves. For understanding this poetics, the formal character of narrative in the mashal, particularly its highly stereotyped nature, is extremely important. For it is precisely in its formulaic, conventionalized character—its outer shape, in other words—that midrashic exegesis discovers its ground of stability, not in an internalized, systematized hermeneutics. Like Rabbinic Judaism itself, the mashal is highly organized without and yet is very free, or at least relatively unregulated, within. In the next chapter, we will consider another midrashic form, the homily, to see how its external character, its language, can deepen our understanding of the midrashic enterprise.

Chapter 3

Forms of Midrash II: Homily and the Language of Exegesis

If the parable is the most distinctive type of narrative in midrash, no mode of discourse is more typical of midrash than the homily, the language of the sermon; and no aspect of midrashic literature raises as many questions as the particular connection between the synagogue sermon and the various exegeses and sermonlike interpretations found in the various midrashic collections. What is the relationship between text and performance in these passages? Are the snippets of sermonlike material or longer homiletical passages found in the midrashic collections transcriptions of actual sermons once delivered in a synagogue or academy? Or are they the literary creations of a redactor, an editor, who wished to preserve for posterity the homiletical material he had in one way or another inherited and collected? Alternatively, is it possible that the collections are actually sourcebooks for preachers, professional manuals containing traditional material that preachers could borrow and work up into their own sermons, not books meant to be read by lay readers? Or are the anthologies really repositories or archives of sermons once delivered but now intended to be studied in the academy by scholar-sages and their students? If so, the collections would have been intended for private readers—not just for a few professional preachers, though still not necessarily for a wider audience of lay readers. What, then, is the relationship between midrash and its audience?[1]

It is not likely that these many questions have a single answer. Indeed, our answers may vary from one midrashic collection to the next, or from one genre of midrash to another. In this chapter, I wish to broach these questions in relation to one major type of midrashic collection. As we shall see, this particular type raises important questions not only about the generic status of the nature of the collection itself—what sort of book it actually is—but also about genre *within* midrash. By this I mean the ways in which midrashic literary forms like the mashal are to be defined, and in particular the ways in which these literary forms create a literary language of their own, thereby achieving the kind of "literariness" I spoke of at the beginning of the last chapter.

The particular type of midrashic collection upon which I wish to concentrate is the homiletical midrash. In the classical period of midrash, this type is represented in two major midrashic works, Vayikra Rabbah, an aggadic midrash on the book of Leviticus, and *Pesikta deRav Kahana*, a collection devoted to the Torah readings on special Sabbaths and holidays in the Jewish year. The interpretations in both collections are mainly attributed to Rabbis of the Amoraic period (third through fifth century C.E.); according to most scholars, the texts of both collections were redacted in the Land of Israel in the late fifth or early sixth century C.E. Vayikra Rabbah was probably edited slightly earlier than *Pesikta deRav Kahana*, but the two collections contain several of the same chapters, and their precise relationship remains a matter of scholarly debate.[2]

The homiletical midrash is one of two types of midrashic collections found in the classical period. The other type of collection, the exegetical anthology, seems to be the chronologically earlier; it is represented by the Tannaitic collections of midrash (named after the Tannaim, the sages who flourished in the second and early third centuries, and whose traditions were probably collected and edited in the late third and fourth centuries) as well as such works as Bereshit Rabbah, the classical Amoraic midrash on Genesis.

The difference between the exegetical and the homiletical collections of midrash is as follows: In the exegetical anthology, interpretive opinions on Scripture are presented in the form of a running commentary on the Bible, verse by verse, often phrase by phrase, without any other clearly discernible logic of organization.[3] By contrast, the homiletical midrash does not offer a continuous exposition of a Scriptural book or passage; instead, each chapter in the collection is devoted to the interpretation of the initial one or two verses in the Torah reading for the week (as the Torah was divided according to the Palestinian triennial cycle in one of its several versions),[4] and those interpretations are themselves organized in a special and apparently conventional structure. That is to say, each chapter is basically composed of two parts. The first of these consists of several proems while the second, more heterogenous in nature than the first, contains various interpretations in different literary forms that comment upon its subject verse (or verses) and sometimes upon topics raised in the course of earlier interpretations; this second part concludes with a peroration that typically invokes the messianic hope or some other consolatory note through the citation of a final verse. We will call this second half the *gufa*, using the term that often marks its beginning as found in the manuscripts of the midrash.

The distinction between the exegetical anthology and the homiletical collection has been a commonplace of Rabbinic scholarship for at least a century.[5] In all this scholarship, however, the difference between the types was treated mainly as a matter of redaction. Only in the early 1970s, in the first of several articles that were among the earliest attempts to explore the significance of midrash as literature, did the Israeli scholar Joseph Heinemann first connect the redactional question to the literary significance of these collections.[6] Heinemann insightfully argued that the separate chapters in Vayikra Rabbah (as well as in *Pesikta deRav Kahana*) possess a coherence deeper than mere external form, a coherence that is a product of literary art. Heinemann characterized this deeper coherence in terms of the organic unity of theme: in his view, each chapter was a carefully chosen group of Rabbinic traditions on a selected topic (for example, the greatness of Moses as a prophet, which Heinemann defined as the theme of the first chapter in Vayikra Rabbah). To describe these chapters, whose redaction he believed was a landmark in the history of midrash, Heinemann coined the term *literary homily* (to distinguish these redactional compositions from oral sermons).

It is difficult today to accept Heinemann's notion of organic unity, both because of the inherent problems with the notion of organic unity and because the so-called literary homilies in Vayikra Rabbah are not usually as unified as they should be, a fact that Heinemann himself acknowledged.[7] Still, I wish to build upon Heinemann's basic insight that the chapters in the homiletical midrash possess literary coherence. Instead of viewing that coherence as deriving from unity of theme, however, I wish to suggest that it lies in a kind of unity of exegesis—that is to say, a shared exegetical approach to the Scriptural verse or verses that serve as the chapter's prooftexts. What "unifies" each chapter, in other words, is a way of reading; and though that way of reading may not be a programmatic effort, it nonetheless reflects a common understanding among the Rabbis whose opinions and interpretations are recorded in the collection. Moreover, that way of reading is exemplified in Vayikra Rabbah especially in the literary form that dominates these collections, the petihta or proem.

For our understanding of the petihta, we are indebted, once again, to Joseph Heinemann.[8] The petihta is an introduction to the lectionary verse that begins the weekly reading from the Torah. According to Heinemann, the petihta originated as a kind of minisermon that the *darshan,* or preacher, delivered in the synagogue immediately before the Torah reading. Just as the *haftarah,* the passage from the Prophets read after the Torah, serves as a kind of epilogue to the Torah reading, so the petihta provides a kind of prologue to it. This putative *Sitz im Leben* for the petihta explains its strange "upside-down" shape. Instead of beginning with its proper subject, the lectionary verse, the petihta opens with another verse—most frequently from the Writings, sometimes from the Prophets, on rare occasions from the Pentateuch—which, to all appearances, is unrelated to the lectionary verse. From this verse, which I will call the petihta verse, the darshan evolves a chain of interpretations, often involving the quotation and interpretation of still other verses along with various other rhetorical devices of interpretation (like parables and enumeration lists), stringing one bead of interpretation upon the next until he arrives at a point where he makes the connection to the lectionary verse, with which the petihta then concludes. At the conclusion, when the lectionary verse is given a new interpretation, some kind of connection between that verse and the opening prooftext can usually be discerned—a word tally, phonetic similarity, or semantic rhyme. Until this point, however, the precise link that the darshan will make between the two verses is not clear. Indeed, according to Heinemann, the darshan would choose the opening petihta verse specifically for its apparent remoteness from the lectionary verse. In this way, he aroused suspense in the members of his audience and made them wonder how he would journey, as it were, from the one verse to the other, the petihta's destination, its telos—the literal end as well as the ultimate determinant for the shape and content of the composition.

Aside from clarifying its rhetorical function, the structure of the petihta exemplifies a fundamental tendency of midrash, the urge to unite the diverse parts of Scripture into a single and seamless whole reflecting the unity of God's will. *Harizah*—stringing verses together as though they were pearls on a necklace—is perhaps the most striking of all Rabbinic exegetical acts. And though it is a tendency that is manifest throughout midrash—at every place two otherwise unconnected verses are joined in order to reveal new nexuses of meaning—the petihta is undoubtedly its most sophisticated literary expression.

As an illustration of this structure, consider the following example, the first petihta in chapter 1 of Vayikra Rabbah. I have labeled its sections for the purpose of the discussion that will follow:

> Rabbi Tanhum ben Rabbi Hanilai began his proem [*patah*]:
> "Bless the Lord, ye messengers [*malakhav*] of His, ye mighty in strength that fulfill His word, hearkening unto the voice of His word" (Ps. 103:20).
>
> A) "Bless the Lord, ye messengers of His": Of what sort does Scripture speak?
>
> 1) If Scripture speaks of those who are above [*ha'elyonim*], does it not also say, "Bless the Lord, all ye hosts of His" (Ps. 103:21)? And if Scripture speaks of those who are below [*hatahtonim*], does it not say, "Bless the Lord, ye angels [literally, messengers] of His" (Ps. 103:20)?
>
> 2) It must therefore be that [*ela*] because those above are [all] able to execute the charges of the Holy One, blessed be He, Scripture says, "Bless the Lord, all ye hosts of His." Because those below cannot [all] execute the charges of the Holy One, blessed be He, Scripture says about them, "Bless the Lord, ye messengers of His," not "*all* ye messengers of His."
>
> 3) Another opinion: Prophets are called *malakhim* [angels]. This is what is written, "And He sent a *malakh* and brought us forth out of Egypt . . ." (Num. 20:16). But was it a *malakh*, an angel? Was it not Moses? Why is he called a *malakh*? But from this source [we learn] that

prophets are called *malakhim*. Similarly, "And the *malakh* of the Lord came up from Gilgal to Bokhim" (Judg. 2:1). But was it a *malakh*, an angel? Was it not Pinhas? So why is he called a *malakh*? Rabbi Simon explained: The face of Pinhas, when the holy spirit rested upon him, flamed like a torch (thus appearing like an angel's face). The Rabbis said: What did Manoah's wife say to her husband?—"A man of God came to me, and his countenance was like the countenance of a *malakh* of God" (Judg. 13:6). She must have thought he was a prophet when he was really an angel! Rabbi Yohanan said: The prophets are called *malakhim* because of their source in Scripture [*mibet av shelahen*]. This is what is written: "Then spoke Haggai, the Lord's *malakh*, in the Lord's messengership [*malakhut*], to the nation, saying" (Hag. 1:13). By necessity you must conclude that because of their origins prophets are called *malakhim*.

B) "Ye mighty in strength that fulfill His word": Of whom does Scripture speak?

Rabbi Isaac said: Scripture speaks of those who observe the sabbatical year [*shomrei shevi'it*]. It is common in the world for a man to perform a precept for a day, or a week, or a month. But for a whole year? And yet this man sees his field untilled, he sees his vineyard untilled, he gives up his living and still he says nothing! Is there a hero [*gibor*] greater than this man?

And if you should argue that this verse does not speak about the observers of the sabbatical year, the proof that it does is that our verse says, "that fulfill His word [*devaro*]," and later it says, "And this is the matter [*davar*] of the sabbatical year's release" (Deut. 15:2). Just as in the latter verse Scripture uses the word *davar* to speak about the observers of the sabbatical year, so in our verse Scripture uses the word *davar* to speak about the observers of the sabbatical year.

C) ". . . ye . . . that fulfill His word, hearkening": Rabbi Huna said in the name of Rabbi Aha: Scripture speaks about the Israelites who stood before Mount Sinai and undertook to "obey and hearken" (Exod. 24:7).

D) "Hearkening unto the voice of His word": Rabbi Tanhum ben Hanilai said: Normally a burden that is heavy for one is light for two. Or if it is heavy for two it is light for four. But is a burden that is too heavy for sixty myriads ever an easy load for a single person? Now all of the Israelites were standing before Mount Sinai, and they said, "If we hear the voice of the Lord our God any longer, then we shall die" (Deut. 5:22). And yet Moses heard the voice of the Lord by himself and he lived! Know that this is so: For out of all of them, the Voice called to Moses alone.

Therefore it is said, "He called unto Moses" (Lev. 1:1).

The lectionary verse for the weekly reading is, of course, the verse with which the petihta concludes, Lev. 1:1, while nearly the entirety of the proem consists of interpretations for its petihta verse, Ps. 103:20. For presenting these latter interpretations, several typical compositional structures are used. In this case, the author of the petihta (perhaps Rabbi Tanhum ben Hanilai, to whom the composition is attributed, but more probably the anonymous redactor of Vayikra Rabbah)[9] uses one of the more common structures, which consists of parsing the petihta verse, Ps. 103:20, into its component phrases, each of which he then identifies with a different subject who is commanded to bless God (as the verse declares). One of the author's motives in doing this is undoubtedly to multiply the number of those who praise God, from the celestial angels above to the peasants observing the sabbatical year below.[10] Once again, though, we can see another major corollary of the Rabbinic ideology of the Torah at work here: namely, the technique of "atomization."[11] Since every verse, indeed every word, in the Torah is divine, it follows that nothing in it, not even a letter or enclitic, is without meaning or purely ornamental. Instead, every word and letter is susceptible to interpretation and, as with the separate phrases in Ps. 103:20, can be exploited as an occasion for interpretation.

In our petihta in Vayikra Rabbah, the interpretations of the different Scriptural phrases and the identification of their subjects, or interpreters, are accomplished mainly by means of word tallies or puns. In addition, nearly all the subjects appear to exemplify a different type of obedience to God and His law. Thus, in the first section (A1–2), the word *malakhim,* which by usage designates angels, is interpreted as referring to earthlings, because the verse stipulates that *all* these creatures cannot obey God's commands, a fact that is not true of angels (who are said to be the subjects of the following verse, Ps. 103:21, which speaks of the heavenly host who do indeed all obey God). The midrash identifies the next phrase in the verse (B) with the *shomrei shevi'it,* the observers of the sabbatical year, paragons of selfless obedience to the law in a time of social and economic crisis.[12] The subsequent phrase, "ye . . . that fulfill His word, hearkening" (C), is ingeniously interpreted as a reference to the children of Israel on the basis of the famous interpretation of Exod. 24:7, according to which they agreed to obey the law even before they heard it. Finally, the last phrase (D) is taken to refer to Moses, who, against all natural logic, was able to endure the divine voice at Sinai and not perish. And so, the petihta concludes, proof of Moses' unique capacity to withstand the burden of God's revelation is confirmed by the fact that God called to Moses "by himself," as it is written, *vayikra el Moshe*. The midrash reads this verse as, in effect, He called to Moses alone.

If this petihta has a single overarching message, it is that God addresses and reveals Himself only to those who have already proved themselves capable of sustaining and enforcing that revelation. This message is most explicit in the petihta's concluding exegesis of Lev. 1:1, and it informs the choice of Ps. 103:20 as the opening petihta verse. This verse appears to have been chosen partly on the basis of a word tally, never made explicit, between the second phrase in our lectionary verse, *vayedaber . . . eilav*, "And He spoke to him," and the word *devaro* in the final phrase in Ps. 103:20, *lishmo'a kol devaro*, "hearkening unto the voice of His word" (which is identified with the Sinaitic revelation, thus forming a parallel to the revelation at the Tent of Meeting, which Lev. 1:1 introduces). The two verses, Ps. 103:20 and Lev. 1:1, join together in a relationship that might almost be described as antiphonal: where Ps. 103:20 enjoins those messengers of God who have heard Him speak to bless Him, Lev. 1:1 describes God calling upon the exemplary messenger, Moses, in order to transmit the law through him to the children of Israel.

This antiphonal relationship, the skeleton of the petihta, determines the exegetical superstructure of the literary form. Yet there also exists within the petihta a second level of exegesis, an infrastructure of interpretation. This level consists of the more elementary exegetical operations that mark every step of the petihta's progress as it moves through its interpretations of Ps. 103:20 until it culminates in Lev. 1:1—the specific exegeses, for example, of the phrases "ye mighty in strength that fulfill His word" or "ye . . . that fulfill His word, hearkening" as well as midrashic traditions, like the exegesis of Exod. 24:7 in C, that are merely alluded to in the petihta and never made explicit. While the superstructure is used to organize the local exegetical options of the infrastructure in order to create the more complex literary form of the petihta, the individual exegeses in the infrastructure are never fully subordinated to the petihta's larger rhetorical strategy. Moreover, in contrast to the superstructure, which serves as the vehicle for the petihta's theme, the interpretations in the infrastructure have no necessary or direct connection to that theme.

To test the relationship between superstructure and infrastructure in the petihta, or between the statement of theme and the pure activity of exegesis, one might consider the place in our petihta of a lengthy digression whose mention I have deferred until now. I am referring to the "other opinion" (*davar aher*) in A3 that identifies the *malakhim* in Ps. 103:20 with prophets, a conventional use of the word in Scripture, for which the midrash offers two lines of explanation. According to the first line, for which several examples are adduced, prophets are called angels because they look like them; according to the second, it is because of the chief passage, Hag. 1:13, their *locus classicus* as it were, that describes the nature of their calling. Now, on strictly exegetical grounds, this "other opinion" is not necessary for the petihta's unfolding interpretation of Ps. 103:20. The part of the verse on which it is based, "ye messengers of His," has already been interpreted in the preceding section.

What, then, is the "other opinion" doing in the petihta? Several explanations are available. First, one might suggest that the "other opinion" is not a genuinely different opinion but simply a further specification of the identity of the earthlings (*hatahtonim*) in the preceding section as prophets. It might also be suggested that the redactor of the homily included the "other opinion" in the petihta because of its relevance to what will later emerge as the homily's two central themes, prophecy (specifically the prophecy of Moses) and language (particularly the relation between name and thing).

Yet even without these explanations, no reader familiar with midrash would ever be bothered by the presence of the "other opinion" in the petihta. The reason for this is simply because there is nothing more common in midrash than another opinion. The "other opinion" represents the basic delight midrash always takes in offering still one more interpretation, no matter what its relevance to the theme at hand may be—which is only to say that in midrash the activity of exegesis is more powerful than the statement of theme. To be sure, the balance between the two is delicate. In the case of the petihta, too lengthy a thematic exposition would swell its shape beyond rhetorical effectiveness; on the other hand, if the exegetical structure is too schematic, the composition ceases to be interesting. But what finally gives the midrashic text its coherence, or semblance thereof, is not thematic unity but the pursuit of interpretation of the Scriptural verse according to the rough linear sequence of its words. So, too, what gives the petihta its coherence as a rhetorical form is the way it seemingly adheres to the exegesis of the petihta verse and nonetheless arrives at its destination in the culminating lectionary verse.

The sense of arriving at a destination, of coming to an end after a journey of some kind, is to a large extent the same impression given by the second half of each chapter in Vayikra Rabbah, the so-called gufa, with its consolatory end and quasi-teleological structure. As I have already noted, the thirty-seven chapters in Vayikra Rabbah share a similar shape. Each chapter begins with one or several petihtaot; all culminate in the same lectionary verse. Perhaps the redactor wished to show that all roads, beginning anywhere in Scripture, lead to a single verse. Perhaps there was a less ideological and more functional reason for preserving multiple petihtaot. In fact, we do not know what practical purposes or functions these collections served. If they were meant to be handbooks or sourcebooks for preachers, the redactor may have wished to give his professional readers a choice of petihtaot from which they could select one as the basis for their Saturday-morning sermon. If the same Torah reading occured only once every three years (on account of the triennial cycle), and if the redactor supplied three petihtaot for that one reading, then a preacher would have to use the same petihta only once every nine years—during which time he could safely assume that his synagogue audience had forgotten the sermon he preached. In any case, following the petihtaot, the gufa then presents a series of further interpretations of the lectionary verse and sometimes of another verse or two (in our chapter, Lev. 1:1 alone), and these interpretations finally culminate in the peroration.[13] Again, we do not know whether these interpretations as a group were meant to serve as material for, or as the basis of, another sermon or a study lesson of some kind, or whether they simply comprise an anthology of related interpretations. What is clear, though, is that the gufa has a definable shape, and that shape is determined by the peroration.

Now this peroration is not simply a *simana denehemta,* a token of consolation the redactor proffers to the reader patiently making his way through the homily to assure him that redemption, too, will arrive sooner or later. Nor is it usually tacked on mechanically to the homiletical interpretations that precede it. Rather, the peroration tends to follow closely upon the earlier interpretations, gathering up meanings that have accumulated in the course of the chapter, often bringing them into sharper focus. In this way, the messianic peroration appears to serve a rhetorical role in the homily that is at least roughly analogous to the one the lectionary verse serves in the petihta: it is a kind of destination, one that has exegetical significance. The peroration verse relates to the chapter's lectionary verse and to the various exegeses that have been given to that verse in the course of the chapter.

Consider the reading, in the first petihta, of *vayikra el Moshe,* "He called unto Moses." I have already translated the petihta's exegesis of the verse as "He called unto Moses alone." This reading is invoked elsewhere in the homily. Moses' unique capacity to endure the divine revelation is raised again in the third petihta, which distinguishes among Moses, Abraham, and David, as well as in the fifth petihta (para. 6). In a later pericope in the gufa (para. 9), Moses is differentiated from Adam, Noah, and Abraham, whom, the midrash concedes, God also addressed directly. Finally, in the last two paragraphs in the homily (paras. 13–14), Gentile prophets are distinguished from their superior Jewish counterparts, and then the latter are distinguished from Moses:

> What was the difference between Moses and all other prophets. . . . The Rabbis say: All the other prophets beheld [God] in a blurred looking glass . . . Moses beheld [Him] in a polished looking glass. . . .
>
> Rabbi Pinhas said in the name of Rabbi Hoshaya: It is like a king who revealed himself to his steward [*ben beito*] in his linen undergarments [*otanin*].[14] For in this world the Divine Presence [*hashekhinah*] reveals itself only to individuals. But in the world-to-come, what is written, "The glory of the Lord shall be revealed, and all the flesh shall see it together, for the mouth of the Lord hath spoken it" (Isa. 30:15).

Thus the peroration: Only in this world does God reveal Himself to individuals like Moses with such casual informality as when a king allows himself to be seen in his undershirt by his personal steward. In the world-to-come, however, God will reveal Himself to all men in this familiar way, and presumably everywhere, not just in the *ohel mo'ed,* the Tent of Meeting, from which God calls Moses in Lev. 1:1.

This interpretation of *vayikra el Moshe* as specifying the uniqueness of the revelation vouchsafed to Moses recurs throughout the chapter. But it is not the sole reading offered for the verse. Even in the passages just cited, the reading always has a nuance unique to the context in which it is presented. Elsewhere in the chapter, the verse is read in such other senses as "God invited Moses into the Tent of Meeting" (para. 7); "He impatiently summoned Moses" (para. 5); "He called attention to Moses" (para. 8); and "He consulted with Moses" (para. 8). Finally, in the second petihta (paras. 2–3), the verse is given still another interpretation, which is absolutely crucial to understanding the chapter's exegetical thrust as a whole. Because the petihta is lengthy, a summary will suffice.

The petihta's prooftext is Hos. 14:8: "They shall return, dwelling under his shadow: they shall make corn grow; they shall blossom as the vine as renowned as the wine of Lebanon." According to Rabbi Abahu, to whom the petihta is attributed, this verse refers to converts to Judaism who come to dwell in the shadow of God. Interpreting the verse's conclusion, Rabbi Abahu reports: "The Holy One, blessed be He, said [*amar hakadosh barukh hu*], 'Dear to Me [*haviv' alai*] are the names of converts as the wine poured before Me upon the altar in the Temple.'" After giving several explanations for why the Temple is called by the name of Lebanon—in a discussion that recalls the passage in the preceding petihta as to why prophets are called *malakhim*—the midrash turns to a second prooftext, 1 Chron. 4:18, which occurs in the midst of the genealogies of the tribes of Israel. For this verse, "and his Judean wife bore Yered, the father of Gedor [*avi Gedor*], Heber, the father of Sokho [*avi Sokho*], and Yekutiel, the father of Zanoah [*avi Zanoah*], and these are the sons of Bityah, the daughter of Pharaoh, whom Mered took," the midrash gives a lengthy interpretation whose gist is as follows: "Yokheved—the mother of Moses—gave birth to a man [e.g., Moses] among whose names are Yered, Avigdor, Heber, Avisokho, Yekutiel, and Avizanoah; and this man was the son of Bityah, the daughter of Pharaoh whom Caleb married." This Bityah is the same daughter of Pharaoh who rescued the infant Moses and named him; according to Rabbinic aggadah, she forsook the idolatry of her fathers, converted to Judaism, and eventually married the famous scout Caleb.[15] Because she rescued Moses and adopted him, the verse calls him her son—a point the midrash then uses to return to the statement it had earlier reported in the name of God: "Dear to Me are the names of converts." This statement is now, in effect, reinterpreted to refer not only to the names the converts themselves bear, but also to the names they give to others. And since Bityah, as Exod. 2:10 reports, "called him by the name of Moses," so, too, *vayikra el Moshe*, "God called him by the name of Moses."

The difference between this reading of the lectionary verse and the others we have seen is obvious. Yet even more significant than its exegetical content is the style of the petihta, its preoccupation with its own virtuosity and exegetical powers, and particularly with its powers of naming and renaming, as can be seen in the exegesis of 1 Chron. 4:18. This verse, like others in the book of Chronicles, served the Rabbis as a favorite ground upon which to let loose all their interpretive energies in free play. Indeed, as several Rabbis were said to have remarked, the book of Chronicles was written in the first place only in order to be interpreted midrashically (*lidareish* [para. 3]).[16]

The object of this exercise in interpretation, however, is not the display of virtuosity for its own sake; rather, it points to a certain kind of language whose nature is suggested by a word repeatedly used in the petihta: *haviv*, a very common adjective in Rabbinic Hebrew, which I have translated as "dear." The root of *haviv* (חבב) occurs only once in the Bible, in Deut. 33:3, in the phrase *af hoveiv amim*, where most commentators understand it to mean "one who loves" or "holds in affection."[17] Indeed, the word *haviv* is cognate to *hibah*, love. The more exact connotation that the word *haviv* has for the Rabbis is suggested by the midrash on the phrase in Deut. 33:3 that is found in the Tannaitic compilation *Sifre Deuteronomy*: "This [verse] teaches that the Lord loved [*havav*] Israel in a way He did not love any other nation or kingdom. . . . This teaches that the Holy One, blessed be He, did not allot His love [*hibah*] to the nations of the world as He alloted it to Israel."[18] Israel's election is a direct consequence of God's *hibah*, and it is God's *hibah* that also bestows upon them their *havivut*, literally preciousness as well as dearness. For the Rabbis, in other words, the word *haviv* connotes a kind of preciousness that derives its special value from the fact of being loved or held in a relationship of affection and intimacy. "Rabbi Akiba used to say: *Havivin* are the people of Israel, for they are called the children of God [*banim lamakom*]" (M. Avot 3:14). Now this assuredly does not mean that the Israelites are literally the children of God. What Rabbi Akiba refers to is not biological filiation but conversionlike affiliation: kinship that is established by intimacy and shared feeling, not by blood; *havivut*, in other words, that derives from familiarity, not from family.

In our petihta, the acknowledgment of precisely this kind of *havivut* produces the act of renaming, which serves, in turn, as the key to the petihta's ultimate interpretation of the lectionary verse. In answering the question of why 1 Chron. 4:18 calls Moses the son of Bityah, Rabbi Joshua of Sikhnin, in the name of Rabbi Levi, reports the following speech that God addressed to Bityah: "The Holy One, blessed be He, said to Bityah: Moses was not your son, and still you called him your son; so, too, you are not my daughter, yet I will call you my daughter"—not Bityah, in other words, but Batyah, literally "the daughter of God." And so, the reader will recall, God's earlier statement in the petihta, "*Haviv* to Me are the names of converts," is given a new meaning: because Bityah/Batyah called her adopted son by the name of Moses (that name being, in fact, a perpetual reminder of the act of *havivut* that established Bityah's special adoptive relationship with Moses when she pulled him out of the river), so, too, God called him by the name of Moses. God Himself adopts this language of *havivut*, of familiarity and intimacy—the language of converts, of those Jews who are called the children of God not by virtue of biological or familial descent but on account of their own act of *havivut*—as His own to speak to His chosen people.

Now in a homily so dominated by a verse that relates how God speaks to a man, the invocation of this language of *havivut* has a special significance. Though it is never explicitly named,[19] this language makes its presence felt throughout the chapter whenever the midrash reports God speaking to Moses, as in the fourth petihta, with its almost tongue-in-cheek portrayal of God's impatience with Moses' legendary (and somewhat wearisome) modesty. Most of all it is felt in the parable that forms the transition to the peroration. In that parable we are told of the time when God will reveal Himself to all men everywhere with precisely the kind of familiarity and intimacy associated with the word *haviv*. In the parable's own imagery, this is the way a king casually reveals himself to his steward, his *ben beito*, literally the son of his house.

Before arriving at that peroration, however, the darshan presents a series of interpretations in the final part of the gufa. These opinions nearly all deal with the second half of the lectionary verse—*vayedaber . . . eilav mei-ohel mo'ed leimor*, "He spoke to him from the Tent of Meeting, saying"—and are especially significant for their literary form. In the final eight paragraphs of the chapter, there are seven complete parables and several quasi-parabolic images. The function of these parables for the most part is praise, their object of praise being either Moses or Jewish prophets in general. Such praise is a common rhetorical function of the parable in midrash.[20] In our present context, however, the praise parable serves not only as a rhetorical device but also as a model of representation. Through parabolic narratives about a human king and his treatment of the members of his court, the darshan is able to represent those situations of intimacy and familiarity between God and Moses (or other Jewish prophets) that characterize the language of *havivut*. The sudden proliferation of parables in the homily points toward the paradoxical fact that God's *havivut* with Israel can be dramatized only through the narrative of human representation.

Such is the literary form of these interpretations. In content, the opinions in the gufa nearly all deal with language and writing or with matters of sequence and relation. Thus, the very first of these opinions (para. 7) raises the question of *semikhut*, of the meaning of the juxtaposition of two unrelated verses, in this case the last verse in the book of Exodus and our lectionary verse, the first in the book of Leviticus. The explanation given for this sequence of verses rests on an analogy between the honor Moses paid to God in building the Tabernacle—an act of honor described explicitly in terms of inscription and writing—and the honor God repaid Moses by inviting him into the Tent of Meeting, that is to say, by speaking to him alone. Following a parable, a series of analogies are drawn between the Tabernacle and the institution of prayer (para. 8). The relevance of the latter to the theme of intimate speech is obvious: prayer is the human analogue to the language of *havivut* in which God addresses mankind. In the next passage (para. 9), the difference between Moses and his predecessors—Adam, Noah, and Abraham (to whom God also spoke)—is explained and confirmed by the citation of Isa. 48:15, a verse in which God announces through the prophet the election of Cyrus as His instrument for Israel's redemption.[21] The invocation of this theme at this point in the homily directly looks forward to the peroration and its evocation of the messianic fulfillment.

In the final section of the gufa, the matter of temporal sequence first raised in the semikhut interpretation reappears in the exegesis offered for the phrase *mei-ohel mo'ed*, "from the Tent of Meeting." Instead of taking the preposition *mei* in a locative sense as designating the place *from which* God addressed Moses, the midrash interprets it temporally as *from the time when* the Tent of Meeting was established. As the midrash proceeds to adumbrate it (paras. 10–12), the significance of this time was charged with ambivalence. This was the time when the law was first publicly promulgated to the children of Israel, thereby making them accountable for its observance. Yet this was also the time when the Divine Voice was first contained within the precincts of the Tent of Meeting. Earlier, when God's voice sounded throughout the world, it so terrified the Earth's inhabitants—that is, the Gentiles—that they could not contain themselves or control their bodily functions. Indeed, the midrash remarks, if the Gentiles had only understood the great benefits the Tent of Meeting conferred upon them, they would have fortified and protected it—and not, as we are surely meant to understand, destroyed the Temple. Finally, this was the time when prophecy ceased among the Gentiles—in other words, when the very nature of divine revelation underwent a radical change, and God chose to address Jews alone. In fact, from this time onward, God directly addressed Moses alone—a fact that distinguishes him from all other Jewish prophets (para. 14)—and solely from within the Tent of Meeting, an unhappy situation but one that will be overturned and corrected in the world-to-come, as the homily's peroration tells us, when God will address all mankind in every place.

The importance of this final section, viewed from the perspective of its culmination in the peroration, is that it decisively alters our sense of the homily's direction. Until the very last pericope, Moses hardly figures in the majority of the interpretations; indeed, their real subject is not Moses but the kind of intimate and familiar discourse, the language of *havivut*, which was first given expression in the petihta about Bityah and functions, as now becomes clear, as a kind of revelatory language in which God addresses man. This language of revelation is not a form of prophecy in the classical sense. Nor is it quite obviously apocalyptic in tenor. It is a private utterance, not a public proclamation, and its significance does not lie so much in its content as in its style—its mode of familiarity. Yet this is the language, our homily tells us, in which God reveals His presence to His messengers. Moses, as the prophet par excellence, exemplifies the man with whom God holds such discourse, but he was not the first man in human history to whom God spoke with such familiarity. He may, however, have been the last—that is, until human history itself ends in the world-to-come.

If the exposition of this language of *havivut* is the purpose of the homily, what was its meaning for the redactor and his audience? The answer to this question is to be found in the overall function that the various exegeses of Lev. 1:1 serve in this chapter. As the reader will have noted, in all these exegeses there is hardly a mention of the laws of sacrifice and of the burnt offering, which form the basis of the greater part of the Torah reading that begins with Lev. 1:1. The reason for this absence, however, is not the intrinsic insusceptibility of this halakhic material to midrash. To the contrary, the Tannaitic midrash on Leviticus, *Sifra*, deals mainly with these laws. Rather, the reason that these laws are not mentioned in Vayikra Rabbah is simply because in the fifth century C.E., nearly four hundred years after the Temple had been destroyed and sacrifices had ceased to be offered, after the aborted attempt to rebuild the Temple under Julian (and when the redactor and his audience probably suspected that the Temple was not likely to be rebuilt in the imminent future), the laws of the Temple cult had little practical import. Confronted by this situation, the redactor of Vayikra Rabbah faced a considerable problem in expounding the Torah reading: why was it significant? If the sacrifices could not actually be performed, what was the point of reading this section in the Torah, let alone studying it? What meaning could these quite substantial sections of the Torah hold for a Jew who could not observe their regulations and prescriptions, however much he may have wanted to do so?

There were, in fact, several Rabbinic solutions to this problem, on both the exegetical and theological planes. One solution was to make the Scriptural passages the objects of intense intellectual and hermeneutical examination; this, for example, is the solution proffered in the Tannaitic midrash *Sifra*, which repeatedly runs the laws of sacrifice in Leviticus through a complicated series of dialectical exercises, as though occupying oneself with the exegesis of the sacrifices was akin to performing them. Another solution was to spiritualize or allegorize the sacrifices—to take the laws of a specific kind of sacrifice, like the meal offering (Lev. 2:1ff.) as emblematic of the poor person who "sacrifices" his or her well-being in order to pay worship to God. Precisely this approach is followed in Vayikra Rabbah itself (in chapter 3), for example. But the particular solution represented in this first chapter of Vayikra

Rabbah was perhaps the most subtle and radical of all. The redactor solved the problem of what to do with this chapter of Leviticus dealing with sacrifices by simply doing the following: He shifted the entire burden of meaning for the reading away from its content, away from the substance of the revelation God addressed to Moses at the Tent of Meeting, that is, the sacrificial laws in all their details, and placed it instead upon the event of revelation and, in particular, the style of its language, the kind of speech that I have attempted to characterize using the term *havivut*. Furthermore, the redactor was able to find a key to this meaning in the lectionary verse, Lev. 1:1. To be sure, most readers would discount the importance of the verse; all it tells us is the identities of the participants in the revelation and its location. Nevertheless, this virtual throwaway line became for the sages in Vayikra Rabbah the very key to salvaging the significance of the Torah reading for their own time. And it was an exegetical significance in Lev. 1:1. After all, the words *vayikra el Moshe* do call attention to the fact that God calls directly upon Moses. The word *vayikra* itself may also have recalled to the redactor the phonetically similar word *yakar*, which like *haviv* means both precious and dear.[22] Finally, the specific meaning the redactor located in the lectionary verse—the language of *havivut*—is, I would propose, suggested in the Torah's own account. If one compares the thunder and lightning of the circumstances surrounding the Sinaitic revelation with the description of the revelation at the Tent of Meeting, the latter is far more prosaic. And yet, to borrow an analogy offered in a parable in our homily (para. 8), just this prosaic quality might have suggested to the rabbis the kind of tête-à-tête, the familiar and confidential interview, a concerned Roman emperor might have held with a trusted provincial administrator over the economic and political situation in a remote Eastern province of the empire.

In this sense, Vayikra Rabbah's exegesis of Lev. 1:1 is a type of interpretation that exemplifies what Paul Ricoeur has described when he speaks of the meaning of the text as "the direction of thought opened up by the text" and of interpretation as "nothing less than an attempt to make estrangement and distanciation productive."[23] Part of the motive for that productivity here may also lie beyond the Scriptural text. E. E. Urbach has argued persuasively that many Rabbinic references to the prophets of the nations, and especially to Balaam (like those in our homily [para. 13]), are to be interpreted as references to Christian Gnostics who claimed to have received ecstatic divine communications.[24] Although the Rabbis vehemently denied the authenticity of these claims, according to Urbach, they may have based their own conceptions of prophecy on the reports of the Christian Gnostics. If we follow the lines suggested by Urbach's argument, the exegesis for Lev. 1:1 in our homily would read: No prophecy God has revealed to anyone, Jew or Gentile, before or after the Tabernacle, has been as intimate or as direct as the prophecy He communicated to Moses (who, it is to be understood, transmitted that prophecy to Israel in the laws of the Torah). On the other hand, the kind of discourse God held with Moses is not inherently vouchsafed to Jews. At the end of days, God will address all mankind in that voice. In the meantime—since Moses and until the world-to-come—the repository of that voice is to be found in midrash, particularly in the way midrash represents God speaking to mankind, not only in homiletical exegeses like those in our chapter from Vayikra Rabbah but also every time midrash makes use of that common yet bold formula *amar hakadosh barukh hu*, "The Holy One, blessed be He, said." Following this formula, God speaks not in the words of Scripture but in the language of midrash's own invention, as if through the mouth of the darshan.[25] Indeed, God's voice in these utterances sounds very much like the voice of the darshan himself. Of course, neither the formula *amar hakadosh barukh hu* in particular nor midrash in general ever lays claim to the authority of classical prophecy. Still, it would be no exaggeration to say that in a time when classical prophecy had ceased among the Jews, the activity of midrash filled a comparable religious need. It helped to restore the sense of God's presence through the discourse of Scriptural exegesis. By joining *havivut* with midrash, a new religious language was created whose very purpose was to reinvoke God as a familiar and intimate presence.

The emergence of this kind of language was not a uniquely Jewish phenomenon. In the Christian sermon, as it was perfected by such early Church Fathers as Augustine (fifth century), a similar kind of language is found in the form of the *sermo humilis*. Like the language of *havivut*, the *sermo humilis* consists in what Erich Auerbach once described as "a new eloquence" capable of encompassing "sublime matters in a lowly or humble style."[26] As Auerbach depicts it, this eloquence eschewed rhetorical virtuosity but used language as an instrument of ethical persuasion, as a means for the preacher to communicate directly with his audience, to teach them, to admonish them, to console them, to give them hope—in short, to directly affect the religious lives of his audience. Like the language of *havivut*, *sermo humilis* is a didactic, homiletical language; its singular power comes from the fact that it never loses sight of the urgency of the lesson it has to teach or the task it must perform.

To be sure, *sermo humilis* and the language of *havivut* are very different as well. As Auerbach has described its development, *sermo humilis* was born out of the confrontation between the rigid stylistic hierarchies of classical rhetoric and the newly egalitarian religious beliefs of early Christianity. According to Auerbach, the conflict between these two systems was epitomized in the word *humilis* with its classical connotations of stylistic lowliness set against the new meaning of spiritual humility it assumed in Christian thought, a humility lowly yet sublime that was thought to be exemplified in the person of Jesus Christ himself. In Rabbinic Judaism, humility as a value or ideal of this sort does not really exist; the value that takes its place is that of modesty, as embodied in those exemplars of modesty, Moses and Hillel. Our own homily tells us (para. 5) that for the latter an act of humbling could also be a form of exultation. Unlike *sermo humilis,* the language of *havivut* is not a language epitomizing humility but the kind of speech God addresses to a modest man like Moses. This language owes its birth not to the breaking of stylistic decorum but to a simpler religious urge, the desire to recreate a sense of God as a familiar and an intimate, a God who still addresses His people between the lines of Scripture—through midrash, in other words—in the absence of a more direct form of revelation.

To describe *havivut* as the language of exegesis (because its origins, as we have seen, are to be found in Scripture, in the second petihta's interpretation of Lev. 1:1) returns us to the question with which we began chapter 2: How can the language and the literature of midrash be described in its own terms? One answer lies in what we have seen in Vayikra Rabbah, in the speech with which the darshan/redactor represents God addressing Israel, that is, in the homiletical discourse that serves here as the medium for midrash. *Havivut* and the homily, like the mashal, might be described as the literary inventions of midrash. *Havivut* represents an attempt to recover God as a speaking presence through literary discourse, and it finds its consummation in the form of the homily, either oral or literary. And just as the language of *havivut* attempts to restore the fullness of divine presence by attributing to God a special way of speaking rather than a particular message with a specific content, so, too, the homily uses the interpretation of Torah as a medium for gaining familiarity and establishing intimacy, of drawing near to God through understanding His law.

The language of homily and the genre of the mashal are two instances of the literariness of midrash. They are also instances of what we might call midrashic *Sondersprache,* "extraordinary speech," language that exceeds the ordinary by becoming startling and memorable in the way that literature always is. To be sure, reading midrash as literature does not necessarily mean reading it just like all other literatures. Midrash is always marked by its singular features: its explicitly exegetical form, which is also its inherent nature; its constant wavering between being a text in its own right and being a commentary on another text; and, together with this wavering, its blurring of the difference between literature and commentary. Finally, midrash is indelibly marked by the religious and theological preoccupations of its authors, the Rabbis, if only because midrash was for them primarily a religious rather than a literary activity. Exactly where those preoccupations enter the picture is a topic we can now begin to broach in the following chapter.

Chapter 4

Midrash and Theology: The Character(s) of God

Our fascination with midrash is not only with its hermeneutic and formal features. Equally powerful is its theological dimension, the range of beliefs that support its exegesis. As the reader will have noticed, nearly all of our discussions in previous chapters have broached questions of theology, of the self-consciously religious import of midrash. These have ranged from the figurative status of Torah in midrash as a kind of metonymy for God to the various spiritualized meanings of the Temple cult that we saw spelled out in the homilies of Vayikra Rabbah. Indeed, as an activity, Torah study—midrash, in other words—was primarily a religious act; as such, its significance was primarily theological.

And yet, as the reader also will have noticed, few steps are more difficult to take—or more prone to error—than the move from exegesis to theology. The problem of deriving the Rabbis' religious beliefs from their commentaries is, in one sense, a mere subset of the larger methodological challenge involved in deriving theme from exegesis and extrapolating a proposition from an interpretation. This problem is complicated in the case of Rabbinic Judaism by the well-known fact, indeed a virtual commonplace of Rabbinic scholarship, that the Rabbis eschewed any sort of systematic theology. They almost never formulated their religious beliefs in any organized way, let alone in a methodological discussion. How, then, does one speak about the theological content of midrash—that is to say, about what the Rabbis believed—without doing violence to the exegetical and programmatically unsystematic character of the literature?

In this chapter, I wish to address that question by considering a topic that is not only a central theological subject in its own right but also one that, perhaps more than any other, encapsulates all the difficulties and problems of discussing Rabbinic theology. The topic is the nature of the divinity. Who did the Rabbis believe God was?

Of all the presences in Rabbinic literature, God's is surely the hardest to pin down. A ubiquitous figure, He defies easy categorization or simple definition. There are several reasons for this. First of all, most of the Rabbis' ideas about God are found in scattered statements of frustrating brevity or in fragments of narrative that must be pieced together to make sense. In either case, the Rabbis' ideas are often cloaked in figurative or imagistic language that requires more than the usual effort of interpretation. Furthermore, although Rabbinic literature does not lack descriptions of God in the predictable terms of divine majesty, supreme power, omniscience, and so on, it is also the case that He is frequently depicted in the most human terms, as a disarmingly familiar figure who acts in ways that often seem improbable for a divinity and are sometimes just plainly inappropriate.

Whenever the Rabbinic conception of God is discussed, it is these latter passages that have traditionally been a major focus of attention, precisely because they pose in its most blatant form the problem of anthropomorphism—the term I will henceforth use as shorthand for all statements that apply human terms and features to describe God's form (anthropomorphism proper) and His feelings (anthropopathism). The Rabbis, of course, did not invent anthropomorphism. Nor were they the first in ancient Jewish literature to employ anthropomorphic language to depict divinity.[1] The Bible is famous for describing God as possessing human limbs like eyes and hands (Gen. 6:8, Exod. 31:28); as acting like a human (walking through the Garden of Eden at noon [Gen. 3:8], regretting having created mankind [Gen. 6:6]); and as having revealed Himself to mankind in human form, as at Sinai with "His feet resting upon the likeness of a pavement of sapphire" (Exod. 24:10), or in the heavenly vision seen by the prophet Ezekiel, in which God is seated upon "the semblance of a throne" in "the semblance of a human form" (Ezek. 1:26).[2]

The Rabbis inherited this literary tradition and, if anything, only intensified its tendencies, exercising their own anthropomorphic imaginations even more boldly than their predecessors. Thus, the Rabbis continued to refer to God as having human limbs and organs (most often in statements so formulaic as to be clichés: for example, as when He is said to point with His finger or swear by His right hand, or when a person is said to be worthy of greeting the face of God's Presence).[3] Even more strikingly, the Rabbis portray God directly in their own image, as putting on tefillin and studying Torah in the heavenly academy, and deciding the law.[4] Most memorably of all, in the many meshalim found in midrash, the Rabbis used the literary genre of the parable to portray God, albeit obliquely, in the form of a human king, who is, as modern scholars have come to recognize, modeled directly upon the known figure of the contemporary Roman emperor or one of his representatives.[5] Far from being generalized or stock representations, mere personifications of God's sovereignty in the world, these portraits of God are vivid, highly particularized depictions of recognizable human figures who frequently act in ways that are shockingly *un*divine: sometimes exhibiting a moving if pathetic vulnerability, at other times acting despotically and unjustly toward their subjects and inferiors. These same features carry over to other nonparabolic narratives in which God figures and acts in ways very different from what one would expect of Him. In one account He is said to weep inconsolably all night over the destruction of the Temple. In another narrative, the famous story of the legal controversy over the "oven of Akhnai," after the sages reject God's own opinion in a legal controversy, He is said to have laughed and exclaimed, "My sons have defeated me, my sons have defeated me."[6]

What does one make of such passages? Traditionally, Rabbinic anthropomorphisms have been discussed mainly with a view to ascertaining the degree to which they reflect the Rabbis' theological beliefs. Did the Rabbis believe that God has an actual human form, and that He is subject to human feelings and emotions, as these passages seem to indicate? Or are these statements that must be understood figuratively rather than literally, precisely because it is assumed as axiomatic that the Rabbis could *never* have believed that God actually possesses a human, let alone a corporeal, form?

These terms of belief, as the matrix for treating the significance of anthropomorphism, were first set by medieval Jewish philosophers. The Rabbis themselves rarely discuss their own use of anthropomorphism, and when they do, it is mainly to extol the use of anthropomorphism in general. "Great is the power of the prophets, for they liken the creature [*tsurah*; literally, form] and its creator [*yotzerah*]," Rabbi Yudan is quoted as saying in Bereshit Rabbah 27:1.[7] And in the one place that the Rabbis discuss the "function" of anthropomorphism (as it appears in the Bible), they ascribe to it what we might call a rhetorical or representational function. Commenting on Amos 3:8—"The lion has roared, who can but fear?"—the *Mekhilta* anonymously asks:

> And who gave strength and force to the lion? Was it not He? But it is merely that we describe [*mekhanin*] Him by [figures derived from] His creatures so as to break open the ear in its capacity for hearing [*leshabeir et haozen mah shehi yekholah lishmoa'*].[8]

What the Rabbis mean by the concluding phrase in the passage is more than simply the apologetic notion that "the Torah speaks in the language of man." Rather, it is closer to the sense of "breaking" the ear "in" to a certain way of hearing, of "opening" its capacities for understanding. This, for them, is the purpose served by the anthropomorphic representation of God. There are no explicit indications in Rabbinic literature of Rabbinic opposition to the use of anthropomorphism.[9]

The first unequivocal evidence of discomfort with anthropomorphism in Jewish literature—that is, the first time that anthropomorphism appears as a problem, as a source of error and misinterpretation—appears only in the early Middle Ages, with Saadiah Gaon, and with the emergence in Judaism of a philosophical conception of God predicated upon the absolute incorporeality, unity, and incomparability of the divine being. To be sure, the real problem for most Jewish philosophers, from Saadiah through Maimonides, was never anthropomorphism per se but the matter of divine attributes, that is, whether any property (especially the so-called essential properties like knowing, loving, and powerfulness) can be predicated of God.[10] Gross anthropomorphisms themselves were less problematic and were understood to be necessarily figurative if only because, taken literally, the statements were so obviously false on philosophical grounds. Even Saadiah sagely acknowledged that "were we, in our effort to give an account of God, to make use only of expressions that are literally true [by which he meant philosophically true] it would be necessary for us to desist from speaking of Him as one that hears and sees and pities and wills to the point where there would be nothing left for us to affirm except the fact of His existence."[11]

Still, the assumptions that led the philosophers to view anthropomorphism as a "problem" have continued to lie beneath virtually every treatment of the phenomenon since the Middle Ages. Most important, they have determined the intellectual framework within which modern scholars have continued to study its meaning, particularly in Rabbinic literature. Whether anthropomorphism has been seen as a problem of metaphysics (the nature of God's being) or of the semantics of religious language (an extreme instance of the question of whether any human expression can truthfully be applied to the description of God), it has nearly always been approached with a view to determining whether or not the Rabbis believed in the literal truth of anthropomorphic statements describing God and His form. Rarely has the phenomenon been approached from the perspective that the Rabbis advocated: anthropomorphism as a literary phenomenon whose significance was primarily rhetorical or representational.[12]

Thus, in his seminal monograph on the "Old Rabbinic Doctrine of God," Arthur Marmorstein collected nearly every Rabbinic statement on anthropomorphism, including exegeses of Biblical verses with anthropomorphic imagery as well as independent formulations, but he did so mainly to identify two distinct "schools" among the early Rabbis, whose development he then traced through later tradition. According to Marmorstein, the first of these schools, associated with Rabbi Akiba, interpreted biblical anthropomorphisms "literally"; the second, the "allegorical" school, connected to the figures of Rabbi Ishmael and Rabbi Yose Hagelili, expressed "a rationalistic point of view" that tended to explain away anthropomorphisms.[13] As Marmorstein showed, the "anthropomorphic trend" gained the upper hand during the Amoraic period, while "a small minority cherished and dared to propogate allegorical doctrines."[14] Only in the Middle Ages did the latter become prominent.

Marmorstein's history is a tour de force of Talmudic erudition. However, its major contention, that two schools with distinctly opposed attitudes to anthropomorphism actually existed, is far from certain. Many of the instances in which Marmorstein claimed to have identified a debate between the "literal" and the "allegorical" schools may actually have been contests over exegetical technique, not anthropomorphism. As H. A. Wolfson noted in discussing Philo, the Rabbis' discomfort with anthropomorphism arose not from philosophical qualms but "out of an inner contradiction which native Jewish speculation could not help noticing in Scripture between its doctrine of the unlikeness of God on the one hand and its use of anthropomorphic descriptions of God on the other."[15] These contradictions were primarily exegetical, not philosophical or theological. Likewise, the motives behind many Rabbinic anthropomorphic interpretations can be shown to be either apologetic or ideological responses to ad hoc occasions rather than discursive propositions about God's being or behavior.[16]

Essentially, Marmorstein read back into Rabbinic literature the later medieval, more philosophically oriented view of anthropomorphism, and then opposed that view to what he called the more conservative "literalism" of Akiba's school. Indeed, as one reads Marmorstein, it gradually becomes clear that his view of Akiba's school and of its literalist view of anthropomorphism has been determined largely by its opponent's position, the more philosophically correct one. More recently, Jacob Neusner has boldly taken up the literalists' side, arguing that one can trace through the history of classic Rabbinic Judaism a growing tendency in favor of anthropomorphism, which reaches its climax with the composition of the Babylonian Talmud. In this work—for Neusner, the acme of Rabbinic Judaism—God is depicted not only anthropomorphically but as incarnate, as having assumed the full particularity of a human being *in the flesh*.[17]

Neusner's audacious claim raises more questions than we can adequately deal with here.[18] For one thing, although many of his examples are drawn from Rabbinic meshalim, he overlooks entirely the parabolic form of these narratives, in particular the intentional obliqueness of the analogy they draw between God and their fictional protagonists. By virtue of that obliqueness, the authors of the meshalim manage to avoid *directly* likening God to human characters, and thus seriously complicate every attempt to interpret such anthropomorphisms *literally*. Still, there exist enough nonparabolic statements that it is imperative for us to take Neusner's strongest argument seriously, namely, his methodological claim for reading all anthropomorphic statements "to mean precisely what they say"—that is, as being "clear evidence of a corporeal conception of God" and not "(merely) poetic characterization, or, indeed, what such a more spiritual interpretation would have required."[19] And indeed, why not read these passages in the most literal fashion—at face value, as it were? Why not argue, as Neusner does, that the Rabbis must have believed that God was a corporeal being, that He was just "like" a human?

The fact of the matter is that, on purely literary and hermeneutical grounds, it is impossible to prove that at least some anthropomorphic statements cannot or should not be read literally. On the other hand, the question of what the Rabbis themselves believed these statements to mean is also unanswerable in any definitive way. In fact, both sides of the case can be plausibly argued. And if the Rabbis did indeed believe that God either possesses or could assume a human shape, they would not have been alone in the world of late antiquity. Belief in the visibility of the gods as well as testimonies to divine appearances in human shape are well documented in pagan religion and literature even in late antiquity.[20] In addition to the enormously complicated controversies in early Christianity concerning the divinity of Jesus' corporeality and his humanity, there are unambiguously anthropomorphic doctrines in early Gnostic texts that may be related in one way or another to esoteric Jewish traditions.[21]

On the other hand, if one compares the pagan or Gnostic sources to the paucity of comparable evidence in Rabbinic literature, or if one compares the extensive documentation surrounding the dogma of Jesus' divinity to the almost total absence of any such discussion in Rabbinic literature, one cannot help but feel the difference between the traditions, and it becomes much more difficult to consider the Rabbinic anthropomorphisms unequivocal and unambiguous sources for belief in God's literal corporeality. Even the one exception to all this, the famous, and famously problematic, document known as *Shi'ur Qomah,* proves the general rule against reading Rabbinic anthropomorphisms literally. The enormous, even monstrous, measurements of God's body recorded in *Shi'ur Qomah* are so fantastic that, as Scholem pointed out long ago, they "have no intelligible meaning or sense-content."[22]

Indeed, before one naively assumes that all anthropomorphisms, graphically detailed though they may be, inevitably presume a belief in divine corporeality and in the material embodiment of God, it is worth remembering that in the late antique world there is no necessary tally between the corporeal body and anthropomorphic language for the body. In a lengthy passage in an early Gnostic text, the *Apocryphon of John,* the narrator describes how the demiurge Ialtabaoth created the first Adam together with his servant "powers," then lists each "power" by name and the limb or organ it created. Yet this Adam, as we learn later in the text, was an entirely "animate"—that is, spiritual—creature; only later is Adam actually embodied in material form.[23] This is, in short, a wholly "spiritual," incorporeal anthropomorphism. To paraphrase Hamlet, there may be more things in heaven and earth than are dreamt of in your modern scholarship.

Finally, and most important, there are powerful and obvious reasons for reading figurative language—or language that appears to be figurative—*figuratively.* These reasons may be difficult to delineate, but that does not diminish their importance. The fact is that the question of God's corporeality is not the most interesting issue raised by the anthromorphic description of God in Rabbinic literature. And when all discussion of anthropomorphism is devoted solely to the matter of corporeality, the more subtle and fascinating nuances of the portrayal of God in human features are simply lost. Yet these nuances may offer the real key to the significance of Rabbinic anthropomorphism. They may actually help us understand how the Rabbis imagined God.

In order to examine these nuances—what we might call the *poetry* of the anthropomorphic analogy—I wish to shift the terms of discussion in this essay from the matrix of belief to that of literary characterization. In other words, I wish to view the anthropomorphic depiction of God as a problem not of belief but of representation, of the construction of divinity, the characterization of God. Anthropomorphism in this view is not just an idiomatic feature of Rabbinic language; nor is it a theological key pointing to God's corporeality or to His attributes. Rather, it is a trope, a case of the figurative use of language to express truth (rather than to obscure or obstruct it, as the philosophical view of anthropomorphism implicitly claims), and a way of exploring the nature of God, of characterizing His behavior.[24] There is real irony, even paradox, behind Rabbinic anthropomorphism, but it has nothing to do with the question of incorporeality. Rather, it is the fact that the only model the Rabbis found complex enough to portray God's character—to communicate the full complexity of *His* nature—was that of a human character, of a human personality. In order to represent God, the Rabbis had no recourse other than anthropomorphism.

As a result, the major question raised by the presence of anthropomorphic statements in Rabbinic literature is not "What did the Rabbis believe about God?" or "How sophisticated was their understanding of God's nature?" or "Did they believe He had a body or not?" but rather "What is God's character? What type of personality does He have?"

To treat the representation of God in Rabbinic literature as a problem of literary characterization is not to demean Him. It is also, I hope, not an anachronism. By calling God a character, I do not mean to suggest that He was either a fiction to the Rabbis or any less an object of worship for them. Quite the opposite: to the extent that the Rabbis were intent upon characterizing God, it was precisely in order to make Him *more* of a God whom they could worship. But the real advantage of viewing God as a character is that it opens up a new perspective from which to consider an old question. By focusing the question upon *how* the Rabbis represent God, upon the representation itself rather than on the beliefs behind the representation, such a study promises to make visible the meaning of Rabbinic representation itself.

Let me offer one example of the kind of new insight that this new perspective holds. When literary theorists speak about character, they tend to use either essentialist or nominalist terms.[25] According to the first approach, character is the product of an essence: a personality, or an "idea" of God. In contrast, for the second approach, character is really no more than a name, a moniker for a locus of functions that a given figure serves in a narrative; aside from its function—the role the "character" plays—the figure does not have an independent existence or identity. Now which of the two conceptions of character more accurately applies to the Rabbinic representation of God? Did the Rabbis possess a coherent sense of God, a theological conception of His nature, or even a number of such conceptions, which they then brought to their various depictions of His behavior and deeds? Or were their portraits of God actually functions of the context in which they appeared, determined more by ad hoc occasional exigencies, exegetical requirements, and particular ideological desires?

Needless to say, these two positions are extreme instances, valuable mainly for heuristic purposes. In fact, the Rabbinic representation of God lies somewhere in between; more accurately, it combines features associated with both approaches (and, to complicate matters further, it resembles one position more closely in some passages and the other elsewhere). Each approach offers an invaluable perspective for viewing Rabbinic representation; however, taken together, they portray God so differently that He seems virtually Janus-faced.

In order to test these two approaches and their separate perspectives on God, I wish to devote the remainder of this chapter to a close analysis of one exceptional text. This text is unique both in its length and for the fullness of its portrayals of God. Preserved as part of the twenty-fourth petihta to Eikhah Rabbah, the classical Amoraic midrashic collection on the book of Lamentations, the text actually consists of two separate narratives, which the anonymous editor of the petihta appears to have joined together because they seem to share a common subject, God's behavior in the aftermath of the destruction of the Second Temple.[26] The lack of real connection between the two narratives is, however, quite evident. In the first place, while the second of the two narratives is attributed to a named sage, Rabbi Samuel ben Nahman, the first one is anonymous. Moreover, the attentive reader will immediately recognize a logical disjunction precisely at the point where the two narratives are joined. Finally, and most tellingly, each of the narratives represents God as having a personality so unlike that found in the other that they are virtual opposites. Indeed, because the God found in each narrative is an entirely distinct character, this text offers a perfect opportunity for exploring the question not only of character but of alternative modes of characterization as well—how different representations may be connected and what their place may be in the overall Rabbinic scheme of things.

In its entirety, petihta 24 consists of a lengthy exegesis of Isa. 22:1–12. The narrative section we will discuss here is found at its very conclusion and comprises the third interpretation given for Isa. 22:12, "The Lord God of Hosts summoned on that day to weeping and lamenting, to tonsuring and girding with sackcloth." For the full text of the narrative, the reader is referred either to the Hebrew original of the petihta or to an English translation.[27] Here I will only summarize the text as I analyze it.

The first of the two narratives begins by telling us that when God initially sought to destroy the Temple, He realized that as long as He was inside the building, His presence protected it. In order to allow the Gentiles to destroy the Temple, God had to remove Himself. He therefore swore not to live in the

Temple[28] until the final redemption. Immediately, the Gentiles invaded the building and destroyed it.

God is trapped, as it were, by the conflicting requirements of His divine powers. Although He wishes to destroy the Temple, His own presence stands in the way, curtailing His freedom to act.[29] To be sure, the notion that God withdrew from the Temple at the time of destruction is not original to Rabbinic aggadah. The idea is suggested in the Bible, specifically in Ezek. 9–11, and it is a motif found in ancient Near Eastern epic and lament, sources that may in some way have influenced the Rabbinic aggadah.[30] In our narrative, however, the motif of withdrawal appears in a somewhat different light. Here it epitomizes a kind of paradox of the divine being, an inherent contradiction in God's literal situation, His presence in the Temple. That location, God's concrete site, is repeatedly emphasized in the language of the narrative. He is described as being genuinely *inside* the Temple. He then takes an oath not to live *there* in the future, and He swears to it "by His right hand," an anthropomorphism whose "veracity" is reemphasized by a midrashic exegesis of Lam. 2:3. And when God finally removes His presence, the Shekhinah, from the Temple, He does so in order to return to His original home—a claim again explicitly confirmed to be "true" through a verse.

In Rabbinic Jadaism, the term *Shekhinah* itself refers to that aspect of God which is closest—both spatially and spiritually—to mankind. Accordingly, most modern commentators explain the motif of the Shekhinah's withdrawal from the Temple as a figure for the exile that God Himself underwent in divine sympathy for His people's plight.[31] As a symbol of God's imminence in the world, the Shekhinah is also an inherently anthropomorphic figure. In fact, its anthropomorphism is precisely the key to the ironic function that it plays at this moment when God releases it—*His* presence—from its dwelling place in the Temple. One would expect the divine presence, once freed from its earthly home, to be freed as well from the travails and sorrows of human existence. In our narrative, though, it is precisely this moment of release that engulfs God in the *figures* of anthropomorphism. From the time He leaves the Temple, God finds Himself hopelessly entrapped in the pathos of human existence, and precisely in the most mortal shapes of that existence: in grief, failure, frailty, senectitude, the presentiment of death.

These confused emotions, all marks of human destiny, successively visit God as the narrative now charts His descent into the depths of mourning. Immediately after He has withdrawn His presence from the Temple, God wakes up to the horrible reality of what has happened—but without, it seems, recognizing His own role in the catastrophe. "What have I done?" He asks Himself. Then, in a series of virtual non sequiturs, He turns angrily upon the Israelite victims of the destruction, at first blaming them for their sins, then for forcing Him to punish them, and finally, as though acknowledging His deepest fear, for giving the Gentiles an opportunity to mock and ridicule Him.

At this point, the archangel Metatron leaps before God and offers to weep in His stead. Presumably the archangel, whose role is to defend the divine majesty, feels that human emotions are beneath God's honor.[32] But the actual effect of the angel's offer to God is to ironize God's own peculiar situation. He refuses to yield to the angel's request. Instead, He insists upon His freedom to weep when and where He pleases. Yet God must still persuade the angel to leave Him, and to do so, He has to threaten Metatron by naming a specific place to which He can withdraw and where the angel cannot enter. The veracity of this "fact" is again confirmed by a verse.

Following this desperate exchange, God's behavior shifts abruptly. He seems constantly on the verge of losing control, of being unable to decide how He feels. After dismissing Metatron, the first thing God does is to order the other angels to go with Him to the Temple to see what the enemy has done—again, as if He does not already know. And the moment God beholds the ruins of the Temple, He breaks into lament. But these laments essentially bewail *His* losses, *His* helplessness, *His* failure to prevent the destruction. "What shall I do for you?" He asks the victims, the Jews whom *He* could not save because (He pointedly tells them) *they* refused to heed His warnings and repent.

Immediately afterward, God turns to the prophet Jeremiah (who, without explanation, suddenly appears in the narrative) and accuses him of failing to show compassion for His plight. This confrontation marks the beginning of God's transformation into both victim and mourner, into the victimized mourner. In one of the narrative's most poignant scenes, God uses the language of the mashal, the Rabbinic parable, to liken Himself to a man who built a wedding chamber for his only son, only to have the son die inside the chamber. The message of this quasi-parable is clear: the son represents Israel, the father God, while the function of the analogy is to elicit consolation and commiseration for God (not, however, for the son). But God will not settle for consolation. He refuses to be consoled. He insists on *not* putting away His grief. His need for consolation is insatiable. Indeed, He is so distraught that He dismisses Jeremiah impatiently, ordering the prophet to summon the patriarchs and Moses because "they," unlike Jeremiah, "know how to weep." After a complicated story describing how Jeremiah finally succeeds in locating the patriarchs, all four ancestors—Abraham, Isaac, Jacob, and Moses—join God in lamenting. In a moment of supreme anthropomorphic imagery, the narrative reaches its climactic conclusion:

> As soon as the Holy One, blessed be He, saw [Moses and the patriarchs], then immediately "The Lord God of Hosts summmoned on that day to weeping and lamenting, to tonsuring and girding with sackcloth" (Isa. 22:12). If it were not explicitly written in Scripture it would be impossible to say it.

They went weeping from one gate to the next, like a man whose deceased kin still lies before him, and the Holy One, blessed be he, lamented, saying: "Woe to that king who triumphed in his youth and who failed in his old age."

The rhetorical complexity of this concluding passage is worth analyzing in detail. What plunges God into full-fledged mourning is the sight of the patriarchs and Moses, the human figures, in mourning. The quotation from Isa. 22:12 is taken literally, as it were, to prove that God actually did call Moses and the patriarchs to mourning, and this interpretation is affirmed by the narrator's gloss, a kind of formulaic qualification whose import is to say that the preceding statement would be unspeakable if Scripture itself had not spoken it. But far from diminishing the force of the anthropomorphism, the effect of the formula is to heighten it, to call attention to the literal sense of the verse. This effect is further strengthened by the simile that the text then invokes to describe God, a simile even more audaciously anthropomorphic than the Scriptural verse. The phrase "like a man whose deceased kin still lies before him" refers specifically to the *onein*, the newly bereaved mourner who has not even had time to bury his deceased relative.[33] According to the halakhah, *aninut*, the state of being an onein, is the most terrible grief a person can suffer; the onein is considered to be so bereft, so shaken by his loss, that he is not required to pray or to observe the positive commandments of the law.

The figure of the onein is a truly radical image for representing God in His grief. Shaken to the very bottom of His self (as it were) by the destruction, the image conveys the degree to which He was literally incapable of assimilating the catastrophe, of absorbing the tragedy in all its horror. And as if this figure were still insufficient, the narrative concludes with an astounding confession that God Himself makes: "Woe to that king who triumphed [*hitsliah*] in his youth and who failed [*lo hitsliah*; literally, did not triumph] in his old age."

Precisely because God is its speaker, this confession cannot be dismissed as merely figurative. And yet, the anthropomorphism in the confession must exceed the purely literal: the confession must be more than a propositional statement about the divine ontology, since, after all, God only *likens* Himself to a human king. What the statement really accomplishes is to return us to the basic ambiguity underlying all anthropomorphic assertions, an ambiguity that is also key to the richness of anthropomorphic language. For the meaning of this confession is surely that God "feels" His old age, whatever that can possibly mean, and that to express such a feeling the author of this narrative had no recourse other than to draw upon the imagery of human feeling. Yet what is so bold about the narrative at this point is that it is not the narrator who describes God anthropomorphically but God Himself. *He* adapts the language of anthromorphism because, stricken by the griefs of humankind, He, too, has no other recourse, no other language in which to express his human, all-too-human, predicament.

The narrative we have just analyzed begins with God withdrawing from the Temple in order to enable its destruction, and it ends with God departing the Temple a second time, but now in mourning. If God begins by mourning the human victims of the destruction, He ends up mourning Himself, His own failure. Indeed, at the conclusion of the narrative, the character of God has so completely identified Himself with the destruction that He has nearly shut out its human victims.

If the character of God in the first narrative is therefore represented in terms of His "closeness," his identification with the destruction—an identification that, by exceeding empathetic sharing, verges upon virtual solipsism—then the mode of His characterization in the second narrative can be formulated in terms of estrangement and distance. In this second narrative, which is a conflation of three separate sources, God is consistently represented as an essentially absent figure—absent, that is, even when He is literally present. He is removed, utterly distant from the narrative's human characters in a way He never is in the first narrative. Thus, where the first narrative ended with God Himself leading the patriarchs and angels in mourning over the destruction, the second narrative opens with Abraham and the angelic host lamenting the destruction while God sits nearby, absolutely oblivious to the scene of lamentation taking place before Him! And when God finally does take notice of the scene, it is only to ask the angels why and what they are lamenting! After this, Abraham asks God why He has inflicted so terrible a punishment upon the people of Israel, and God replies matter-of-factly that the people of Israel deserved their punishment on account of their sins. In His reply, it is worth noting, there is not a hint of any concern for the Jews, let alone any pain or compassion for their unhappy situation.[34]

At this point, the narrative turns into a trial in which God, acting simultaneously as judge and prosecutor, calls witnesses to testify to Israel's transgressions. The first witness is the Torah, and she is followed by the successive letters of the Hebrew alphabet. Abraham, however, manages to dissuade each witness from testifying until, finally, God has no one else to subpoena.

In the next section of the narrative, the three patriarchs and Moses appeal to God to show mercy to Israel. Each figure cites the great deeds he performed in the past to plead Israel's case, but their pleas have no effect upon God, who remains silent, utterly impassive, unmoved. As the narrative proceeds, plea by plea, with no response from God, His obduracy and lack of feeling become almost painful to observe. The sense of His absence is palpable to the other characters—the human characters—in the narrative as well, and so Moses, as though he knows God will do nothing, decides to go with Jeremiah to visit the Jews in exile so that someone might at least offer them consolation. Initially, in fact, Moses appears determined to redeem the Jews by himself, but a Heavenly Voice stops him by announcing that the Jews' punishment and their exile are divine decrees. This Heavenly Voice is the single audible token of divine intervention to be recorded in the entire second narrative.

After returning to the patriarchs, Moses addresses a series of laments: to the sun, to the Temple, to the Gentile enemy. Addressing the last group, the Gentiles, he implores them not to be unnecessarily cruel to their Jewish victims; yet, as the narrator grimly reminds us, the Babylonians did not heed Moses' request. Only at this point does Moses finally address God directly. But his speech is now a complaint against God's behavior: How, Moses asks, could God have remained silent while the Gentiles slaughtered Jewish children in the presence of their mothers? How could God have done this when He Himself, in Lev. 22:28, forbids Jews to kill animals in this way? God, Moses charges, has acted contrary to His own law.[35] Yet God still remains silent; he does not reply even to this complaint.

Finally, in the last section of the narrative, after all the male figures in Israel's past have failed to move God, the matriarch Rachel rises on Israel's behalf. Like the patriarchs who preceded her, Rachel invokes her past deeds; yet unlike them, she recounts one deed that was less famously exemplary. Rachel tells God the story of how she conquered her jealousy when she went along with her conniving father Laban in tricking Jacob on their intended wedding night, helping her sister Leah take her place in Jacob's bed and thus become his wife. Why did she do this? In order, she tells God, to prevent Leah from being disgraced and shamed. Yet how, Rachel demands of God, can He let His jealousy, which is solely jealousy of idols, prevent Him from showing compassion to the people of Israel? How can such petty jealousy on His part justify Israel's great shame and their national disgrace?

Amazingly, this argument finally succeeds in moving God. Yielding to Rachel, He agrees to show mercy to Israel and promises to restore them. This promise is confirmed by Jer. 31:15–17, the two verses with which the passage concludes.

This climactic scene is no doubt the most powerful in the entire text. What is so powerful about it is the sight of God yielding to Rachel, of His masculine hardness submitting to the compassionate softness of the matriarch's plea. Indeed, it would be tempting to interpret this scene, with its wholly unanticipated change in God's heart, as affirming the emergence of a feminine presence *within* God Himself, a kind of *dea ex machina*.[36] The opposite, however, is true. Once again, we observe the narrative reverting to the anthropomorphic paradox. For while Rachel's gender does possess a symbolic meaning, it is not that of divinity; rather, her gender epitomizes humanity while God's utter masculinity is the mark of divinity. By allowing Himself to be persuaded by a female's argument, God does not Himself become feminine. Rather, in an ironic reversal of *imitatio dei* that we might call *imitatio hominis*, it is the model of *human* behavior to which God now turns.[37] By submitting to Rachel's example, to her acknowledgment of her own jealousy, God is now able to acknowledge His jealousy, and He is able to extend mercy to Israel.

The notion of *imitatio hominis* has parallels elsewhere in Rabbinic literature, even in Eikhah Rabbah itself.[38] In this narrative, however, God's imitation of human behavior represents more than an anthropomorphic trope writ large. It also implies a devastating critique of God's past deeds. All His wrath, we now learn, has been fueled by mere jealousy, by envy of idols that, as Rachel reminds Him, do not even possess "substance." God, in His own words, has been jealous of literally nothing, and Israel, therefore, has suffered on account of literally nothing. God's jealousy, one might say, is beneath pettiness. Even when God finally acknowledges this pettiness and puts aside His anger, the sole motive for this change of heart seems to be shame at being found out to be so petty. There is no indication that He feels any real concern or honest compassion for the Jews' plight.

The character of God presented in this second narrative is therefore the virtual opposite of the God in the first narrative. This God is characterized by a stony, disturbingly cold detachment from His nation and their travails. In contrast to the God of the first narrative, whose personal identification with the destruction was nearly total, this God is entirely indifferent to the sufferings of his nation. Indeed, it is hard to think of two characters more different than these two Gods. All they seem to share is a name.

What can we make of these two characters of God? And what is their relationship to each other? As I proposed earlier, the literary concept of character can be considered in either essentialist or nominalist terms. Which of these is more helpful for understanding our two characterizations? Do their anthropomorphic portraits of God derive from a preconceived theological "view" or a preconception of His "psyche" (the latter term itself a vast anthropomorphism)? Or are the traits of God's personalities, as depicted in the two narratives, functions of the roles He is made to serve in each, products of local pressures (exegetical, ideological, etc.) and their requirements?

We can begin with the essentialist perspective. First of all, the simple fact that the two narratives present full-blown yet diametrically opposed characterizations of God, each of which could stand alone, clearly indicates that a single "essence"—either conceptual or psychological—from which both characterizations directly derived does not exist. On the other hand, as students of Rabbinic thought know all too well, the Rabbis' concept of God is typically expressed in terms of paired features—justice and mercy, or transcendence and immanence, for example. Might some version of these paired features have been the model for our two characterizations?

Justice and mercy, as represented in the two attributes *middat hadin* and *middat harahamim*, would at first appear to be the most likely candidates.[39] But neither of these attributes represents a truly appropriate category for either characterization. For one thing, our two representations of God are more like caricatures of Justice and Mercy than fitting personifications of the abstract principles. Morever, the two *middot,* as attributes of the divine being, derive their real meaning from their struggle *within* God. While *middat hadin* is occasionally hypostatized as the infamous *kateigor,* the Satanlike prosecutor of Israel (we will look at one such occasion shortly), the attributes as a pair are rarely fully independent beings.

Similarly, the two divine characterizations are far from being personifications of God's transcendence or immanence. These are the categories that E. E. Urbach, in his magisterial presentation in *The Sages,* uses to define the Rabbinic God who oscillates between absolute otherness on the one side and closeness to mankind on the other.[40] In Urbach's view, the Rabbis, insistent that God not be identified with nature or with the phenomenal world and yet equally determined to maintain His providential connectedness with this world, walked a kind of tightrope between heaven and earth. That tightrope was anthropomorphism, the literary corollary for the Rabbis' desire to uphold the side of immanence. By representing God with human features, they affirmed His abiding concern with the world of humanity.

It is certainly true that the attributes of transcendence and immanence also play into the characterizations we have analyzed. And yet, the abstract attributes do not really explain the precise features of the two *characters* that emerge in the narratives, or their genesis. For what distinguishes those characterizations—what makes them into viable characters—is not their transcendence or immanence but their humanlike behavior in all its unpredictability and strangeness. That behavior, the core of the anthropomorphic impulse in each narrative, is not a functional device or strategy serving a higher purpose, as Urbach maintains, but the characters' very mode of representation, even self-representation. This can be seen most clearly when, in each narrative, God Himself undertakes to imitate human behavior, to adopt the anthropomorphic turn for Himself. In each case, God's intention is not to demonstrate His abiding concern with mankind. He imitates human behavior because He has no other satisfactory model to instruct Him as to how He should behave.

Our two divine characters do not directly derive, then, from any of these conventional theological categories for the Rabbinic God. But might the characters be the products of a more specific, local need, an exegetical impulse, for example? In our text this is, unfortunately, not the case. For while the two narratives both use Scriptural verses to prove their anthropomorphic claims at different points, the narratives themselves do not seem to be exegetical artifacts. On the other hand, it is certainly fair to suggest that the extreme nature of the two characterizations of God—the very feature that all but makes them into caricatures—may very well have derived from the equally extreme, radically catastrophic nature of the historical event that serves as their backdrop and overall context, namely, the destruction of the Temple. Each portrait of God reflects in some way what must have been the deepest feelings Jews experienced in the aftermath of the destruction:

extreme guilt on the one hand, as though the catastrophe had been entirely deserved on account of their great sins, and extreme self-pity on the other, as though the catastrophe had been wholly undeserved since it far exceeded any transgression they could have committed to warrant such punishment.

The pressures exerted by these feelings may help us to understand the tone of near-desperation that lies behind both narratives. That tone also points to a mythic quality both narratives share despite the different ways they represent God. The same mythic quality is found in some other Rabbinic passages that portray God. Consider, for example, the following section from Bereshit Rabbah 8:3. The passage is taken from a lengthy series of interpretations, all of which are devoted to the problematic phrase in Gen. 1:26: "And God said, 'Let us make man. . . .'" One of several questions that this problematic verse posed for ancient Jewish exegetes was: Whom did God consult when He said, "Let *us* . . . "? The following are two answers offered in the midrash.

> Rabbi Berechiah said: When the Holy One, blessed be He, was about to create Adam, He foresaw that both righteous and wicked descendants would issue forth from him. He said: If I create him, then wicked men will come forth from him. But if I don't create him, how will the righteous come into existence? So what did the Holy One, blessed be He, do? He removed the ways of the wicked from before Him, and joined with the Attribute of Mercy, and created man. This is what the verse [means]: "For the Lord cherishes the way of the righteous, but the way of the wicked will perish [*toveid*]" (Ps. 1:6). What does *toveid* mean? He made it perish [*ibedah*] from before Him, and joined with the Attribute of Mercy [*middat harahamim*], and created man.
>
> Rabbi Hanina did not say thus, but: When the Holy One, blessed be He, was about to create Adam, He took counsel with the ministering angels. They asked Him: What is [man's] character? He answered: Righteous men will issue forth from him. That is what the verse [means:] "For the Lord cherishes [*yodei'a*, literally, knows] the way of the righteous" (Ps. 1:6)—[this means:] God made known [*hodi'a*] the way of the righteous to the ministering angels. " . . . but the way of the wicked will perish [*toveid*]" (Ps. 1:6)—[this means:] He made it perish from before them. He revealed to the angels that the righteous would issue from Adam, but He did not reveal to them that the wicked would issue forth as well. For if He had revealed to them that the wicked would issue forth from him, the Attribute of Justice [*middat hadin*] would not have allowed him to be created.

The first thing to note about this passage is that what looks like a real exchange between two sages, Rabbi Berechiah and Rabbi Hanina, is actually an editorial invention: Rabbi Hanina, a first-generation Amorah, could never actually have responded to Rabbi Berechiah, a sage who lived some four generations later.[41] Still, what Rabbi Hanina *would* have found objectionable in Rabbi Berechiah's interpretation is the idea that God created man with a partner, even one so closely identified with Him as the Attribute of Mercy. The major difference between Rabbi Berechiah's interpretation and Rabbi Hanina's alternative is that, in the latter, God creates man entirely by Himself; whomever He happened to consult He talked to before He actually created man. Therefore, when the verse says, "Let *us* make man," it refers merely to that preliminary consultation.

The source of Rabbi Hanina's discomfort with his colleague's interpretation is doubtless his fear that someone might use the verse to prove the existence of a second divinity in heaven. This could be either a Logoslike hypostasis or a Gnostic *demiourgos*. Rabbi Hanina's interpretation effectively rules out that possibility. Yet it is worth considering the "price" he must pay to accomplish this ideological end—that is, the representational price in characterizing God. For if Hanina's interpretation eliminates the possibility of someone finding a second divinity in the verse, it is predicated upon a deeply anthropomorphic characterization of God.

True, even in Rabbi Berechiah's interpretation, there is a nascent anthropomorphism present in the motif of God putting aside His knowledge (of the eventual existence of the wicked) from Himself (literally, "from before His face") so as to be able to create man. In Hanina's opinion, however, this anthropomorphic conceit is blown up into a full character trait. According to Hanina, God does not simply hide His knowledge from Himself. He acts deceptively. He conceals what He knows from the angels. And why? Because He knows that the Attribute of Justice, if it knew the whole truth, "would not have allowed Him to create man." Aside from the fact that the Attribute of Justice appears here as a full-fledged hypostasis, as a being virtually distinct from God (precisely the kind of presence Hanina wished to exclude from the interpretation), the attribute is now a figure who appears to be more powerful than God Himself. As a character in its own right, the attribute resembles the mythological Moira, or Fate, whose decrees even the gods cannot overrule. For good reason God is afraid, and He feels that He must hide His knowledge from the attribute and create man on the sly.

There are, to be sure, any number of logical and theological objections one might raise against this narrative (and, for that matter, against Berechiah's interpretation as well). How can God hide something from Himself? How can He hide something from the Attribute of Justice if it is so powerful? And if it is so powerful, how can it not know what God knows? Besides, what good is hiding the knowledge? Won't the truth eventually come out? These are all good theological questions, but they are not really relevant to understanding the narrative, precisely because its meaning rests not upon logical or theological consistency but upon the force of its characterization of God. And, as in our Eikhah Rabbah petihta, what makes this characterization of God so compelling is its felt interiority, the sense it gives of representing a wholly recognizable psyche or self.

In the case of these two narrative interpretations of Gen. 1:26, can we say what the model for God's character or psyche might be? In part, as we have seen, the impetus for the characterization is exegetical, a combination of the textual and ideological difficulties posed by the problematic phrase in Gen. 1:26. In addition, though, Hanina's portrayal of God, like that of the king in the Rabbinic mashal, appears to be modeled on the Roman emperor (or one of his representatives in Palestine). But this king is hardly the *kosmokrator,* an unperturbed, omnipotent world ruler. Rather, he is a beleaguered, often browbeaten figure, perhaps possessed of absolute power, but either corrupted by that power or unsure about how to use it confidently. He is afraid of his very own counselors and subordinates—figures like Metatron or the *middat hadin* or the angels, who sometimes act more like a bunch of insubordinate, Sejanuslike conspirators than loyal freedmen, God's *familia*. This king, in other words, is not so much ruler as ruled—by the imperial bureaucracy, by his anxieties about losing power, by his own fears.[42] The same model also seems to partially inform the tragic, solipsistic character of the defeated God in the lengthy first narrative from Eikhah Rabbah, and perhaps even the heartless despot of the second narrative. Even there He is not quite the truly imperious ruler He would like to imagine Himself. After all, Rachel persuades Him to change His mind by forcing Him to recognize His "justice" for what it really is—vanity and petty jealousy.

The recognition of this imperial model for the Rabbis' portrait of God is significant for several reasons. First, it suggests how deeply rooted in history, in their own historical moment, was their construction of God. Of course, the representation of God as king was in no way an innovation of the Rabbis. The image of God as king has a venerable history going back to the earliest texts of ancient Near Eastern literature, and it is a virtual cliché in the Bible.[43] It is not surprising that the Rabbis should have chosen this conventional figure for power and sovereignty as their symbolic figure for God. What is revealing, though, is that the model they selected should have been a king so insecure and lacking confidence in his ability to exercise the power at his disposal. In portraying God this way, the Rabbis were surely mirroring their own feelings of insecurity, their own self-conscious powerlessness in the world, and their anger and resentment at the earthly powers who controlled their this-worldly existence. The Rabbis' God, in other words, offered them no refuge from the world; He was too much like that world.

In light of their common roots in this imperial model, the differences between the two characters of God portrayed in the Eikhah Rabbah petihta may also seem somewhat less pronounced. The imperial model certainly does not explain the differences between the characterizations. And quite obviously, the imperial model was not the only model the Rabbis had available to construct divinity.

Indeed, what is needed is an inventory of the characterizations of God throughout Rabbinic literature, from the God of mercy to God the trickster. Only with such an inventory in hand could we determine if the two characterizations of God in Eikhah Rabbah are truly exceptional, whether they are representative portaits, or whether they are merely two types along a spectrum of divine characterizations. But if we return to our earlier terminology, we can say that while the imperial model points to an essentialist approach to character, the specific features of the separate portrayals of God require the nominalist approach to explain them. We will need to concentrate more fully on the functions each divinity serves and the roles each divinity is called upon to play in its respective narrative. It is impossible to understand these characters outside their narratives, just as it is impossible to imagine one divinity appearing in the other's narrative: that is, the God of the first narrative acting as the judge in the trial in the second narrative, or the God of the second narrative bemoaning His tribulation in words like "I succeeded in my youth and failed in my old age." Each character is fully rooted in its own story. The anthropomorphic construction of God is always a presence within a narrative or a larger aggadah (even if those narratives and aggadot are preserved only in fragments). As a character, God hardly ever appears in Rabbinic literature in isolation, as the object of independent discourse; He is always doing *something*, always part of some story in which He plays some role.

This last point may help us to reconsider a question raised earlier, the question of the Rabbis' beliefs about God. If God is a character whose meaning cannot be discussed apart from the narratives in which He appears, then the question "What did the Rabbis believe when they depicted God anthropomorphically?" cannot be answered without asking, "What did the Rabbis believe about their aggadot?" Did they believe they were historically veracious, that they occurred as narrated? If they believed that God actually possessed the anthropomorphic features attributed to Him in the aggadot, did they also believe in all the other details and incidents in these narratives as well? When they described God sitting in judgment in heaven (as in the second Eikhah Rabbah narrative), they surely had no difficulty believing that the patriarchs and matriarchs were there, pleading for Israel before God. But did they also believe that the Torah and its letters spoke and acted like persons, refusing to testify against Israel, as the aggadah says they did? Did they also accept these personifications at face value?

Far more so than biblical narrative, Rabbinic aggadah resembles ancient Greco-Roman myth, a tradition that remained very much alive in late antiquity.[44] Consequently, the question "Did the Rabbis believe in their aggadot?" is not very different from the question "Did the Greeks believe in their myths?" Precisely this question has been asked by the French classicist Paul Veyne.[45] The general subjects of Veyne's book are Greek and Roman authors from Herodotus on, but Veyne's real concern is with late antique figures like the second-century traveler and geographer Pausanias. In his accounts of various localities and their cults, Pausanias, Veyne notes, simultaneously seems to be skeptical of the traditional myths and yet willing to entertain them as possessing some kind of truth. For Veyne, Pausanias's position personifies the ancients' dilemma of belief:

> The Greeks believe and do not believe in their myths. They believe in them, but they use them and cease believing at the point where their interest in believing ends. It should be added in their defense that their bad faith resided in their belief rather than in their ulterior motives. Myth was nothing more than a superstition of the half-literate, which the learned called into question. The co-existence of contradictory truths in the same mind is nonetheless a universal fact.[46]

To be sure, the Rabbis never exhibit precisely the same kind of skepticism about aggadah as do writers like Pausanias (though there are exchanges such as the famous one between Akiba and Eleazar ben Azariah over the singular "frog" in Exod. 8:2 [Shemot Rabbah 10:4] that suggest a boundary did exist between the credible and the incredible). But what is most valuable about Veyne's approach to the question of ancient belief is less the direct connection of myth to aggadah than the grounds for belief in myth that Veyne attempts to establish. According to Veyne, myths, first of all, tend to be anonymous; this is frequently true of aggadah (even when a given aggadah is attributed). Inasmuch as aggadah in general represents an oral tradition, the "author" is frequently just a tradent, one who transmitted a tradition from his teachers. Second, myths repeat what was already said: "When it comes to gods and heroes, the only source of knowledge is the 'they say,' and this source has a mysterious authority."[47] That authority is not unlike the authority of Scripture as it is invoked by exegetes in aggadah, most obviously when a text records "as it is written," but perhaps even more so in such expressions as "if Scripture did not say it, it would be impossible to believe." Far from being an apology for anthropomorphism, as the expression is generally understood, it may actually be seen as an appeal to authority in order to gain credibility.

Third, and most important, there is what Veyne calls the sense of a "time of myths," of a "mythological space and time . . . secretly different from our own." Veyne astutely describes this sense:

> A Greek put the gods "in heaven," but he would have been astounded to see them in the sky. He would have been no less astounded, if someone, using time in its literal sense, told him that Hephaestus had just remarried or that Athena had aged a great deal lately. Then he would have realized that in his own eyes mythic time had only a vague analogy with daily temporality; he

> would also have thought that a kind of lethargy had always kept him from recognizing this difference.[48]

One could easily identify an analogous "aggadic time and space," different not only from our own time but from that in which the Rabbis themselves lived. For the most part, that aggadic time and space would have been coeval with the world of the biblical past—a distant, self-encapsulated past for the Rabbis—but it may very well have included the entire period of the Temple's existence, right up until the destruction, the event the Rabbis considered the true historical watershed, the time when earlier history ended and their own began (and the time precisely when the two narratives in Eikhah Rabbah are said to transpire).[49]

Whenever it was believed to have ended, the time and space of aggadah, like that of myth, encompassed a world in which God could act and behave anthropomorphically. This does not mean that the Rabbis would necessarily have responded affirmatively if someone had asked them if God were a person just like themselves. They probably would have responded that the personhood of God was only vaguely analogous to personhood in their world as they knew it from their daily lives. And it was precisely in that vaguely analogous way that they believed in the anthropomorphic description of God.

Midrash and aggadah are, of course, very closely connected. And if the Rabbis had been asked if they believed in the "truth" of midrash—of the interpretations the Rabbis offered, which implicitly or explicitly contain aggadot that raise the same kinds of problems for us as do the Rabbis' various anthropomorphic descriptions of God, or which refer to incidents or characters nowhere to be found in the Bible—they would probably have offered a similar answer: that the midrashim were true but that their truth was hardly the same truth as the kind they might have encountered in their daily lives. This is probably as close as we will ever come to knowing what the Rabbis believed. And there is no reason for us, the Rabbis' modern readers, to believe more or less than they did.

Notes

Introduction

1. Geoffrey Hartman, "Criticism and Restitution," *Tikkun* 4, no. 1 (1989): 31.

2. *Midrash and Literature*, ed. Hartman and Sanford Budick (New Haven, Conn., 1986). It is worth noting that even this seminar, although it took place in Jerusalem, was largely an American affair. The initiative for it came from the university's Center for Literary Study, which was largely an adjunct to its Department of English, composed of primarily American or American-trained faculty. Participation of faculty from the School of Jewish Studies, though not wholly lacking, was decidedly minimal.

3. G. Douglas Atkins, "Dehellenizing Literary Criticism," *College English* 41 (1980): 769–79.

4. On the Bible-as-literature movement, see Robert Alter, *The World of Biblical Literature* (New York, 1991), esp. pp. 1–24 and 191–210; Meir Sternberg, *The Poetics of Biblical Narrative: Ideological Literature and the Drama of Reading* (Bloomington, Ind., 1985).

5. To name only a few of the most important works: Daniel Boyarin, *Intertextuality and the Reading of Midrash* (Bloomington, Ind., 1990); Boyarin, *Carnal Israel: Reading Sex in Talmudic Culture* (Berkeley and Los Angeles, 1993); Jose Faur, *Golden Doves with Silver Dots: Semiotics and Textuality in Rabbinic Tradition* (Bloomington, Ind., 1986); Steven D. Fraade, *From Tradition to Commentary: Torah and Its Interpretation in the Midrash Sifre to Deuteronomy* (Albany, 1991); James L. Kugel, *In Potiphar's House: The Interpretive Life of Biblical Texts* (San Francisco, 1990); Michael Fishbane, *The Garments of Torah: Essays in Biblical Hermeneutics* (Bloomington, Ind., 1989); David Stern, *Parables in Midrash: Narrative and Exegesis in Rabbinic Literature* (Cambridge, Mass., 1991).

6. See, for example, Martin Jaffee's review of Boyarin's *Intertextuality and the Reading of Midrash*: "The Hermeneutical Model of Midrashic Studies: What It Reveals and What It Conceals," *Prooftexts* 11 (1991): 67–76. Jaffee raises the question of the relationship between theoretical studies of midrash like Boyarin's and the work of Jacob Neusner, particularly his approach to Rabbinic literature as a series of discrete "documents," each coherent in its own right and each providing autonomous testimony to a different representation of Judaism in its historical development, even within the Rabbinic period. Like the theoretical studies discussed in this introduction, Neusner's work has challenged the traditional modes of Rabbinic scholarship, and any study of Rabbinic scholarship in this century would surely

have to deal with Neusner's enormous corpus in detail. However, the impact of his work on the midrash-theory connection has been, for better or worse, minimal, so I have chosen not to discuss his methods or conclusions here. Specific points relating to his work are taken up in chapters 3 and 4.

7. The outstanding example of this argument is Susan A. Handelman's *The Slayers of Moses: The Emergence of Rabbinic Interpretation in Modern Literary Theory* (Albany, 1982). See also Stern, "Moses-cide: Midrash and Contemporary Literary Criticism," *Prooftexts* 4 (1984): 193–213.

8. See Herbert Schneidau, *Sacred Discontent: The Bible and Western Tradition* (1976; Berkeley and Los Angeles, 1977); Schneidau, "The Word Against the Word: Derrida on Textuality," *Semeia* 23 (1982): 5–28, and the other articles in that issue, a special issue on "Derrida and Biblical Studies."

9. The literature on Hellenism and Rabbinic Judaism is vast. The classic works are those of Saul Lieberman, *Greek in Jewish Palestine* (New York, 1942), and *Hellenism in Jewish Palestine* (New York, 1950). For some sense of the contributions and bibliography in the first three-quarters of this century, see Henry Fischel, *Essays in Greco-Roman and Related Talmudic Literature* (New York, 1977).

10. See Elisa New, "Pharaoh's Birthstool: Deconstruction and Midrash," *Sub-Stance* 57 (1988): 26–36. New's stunning article is itself symptomatic of the problem it so brilliantly analyzes: the centerpiece of her essay is a wonderfully insightful comparative analysis of a passage from Geoffrey Hartman's *Criticism in the Wilderness* with a passage from Shemot (Exodus) Rabbah; what New never realizes, however, is that the midrashic passage is textually corrupt and its meaning therefore unclear.

11. Leopold Zunz, *Die gottesdienstlichen Vortraege der Juden historisch entwickelt*, (1832; Frankfurt, 1892). Translated into Hebrew and supplemented by Chanoch Albeck as *Haderashot Beyisrael* (Jerusalem, 1954).

12. Yitzhak Heinemann, *Darkhei ha'aggadah*, 3d ed. (Jerusalem, 1970); Max Kadushin, *The Rabbinic Mind* (New York, 1952); Joseph Heinemann, *Aggadot Vetoldoteihen* (Jerusalem, 1974). For further references, see chapter 3 note 6.

13. Indeed, part of the reason why midrash found a place for itself within a Hebrew literature department was simply because the academic study of Talmud was (and to a large extent still remains) almost purely philological and historical. The kind of study midrash requires—both formal and thematic—did not always fit easily into the departmental setting of Talmudic studies, which was generally devoted to the more "rigorous" areas of Talmud and halakhah, Rabbinic law and its literature. By placing the study of midrash and aggadah in the department of Hebrew literature, the age-old competition of midrash and Talmud, aggadah and halakhah, was in fact being reenacted.

14. This was part of the legacy of Hayyim Nahman Bialik and Yehoshua Hana Ravnitzky's monumetal *Sefer Haaggadah* (Odessa, 1908–11; rev. ed., Tel Aviv, 1936;

2d rev. ed., 1952). See my introduction to the English translation: *The Book of Legends: Sefer Ha-Aggadah*, trans. William G. Braude (New York, 1992), pp. xvii–xxii.

15. Hartman's work on Jewish texts remains to be collected and in some cases—such as some of his lectures on midrash—published. See, however, "Criticism and Restitution"; "The Struggle for the Text," in *Midrash and Literature*, pp. 3–18; "Imagination," in *Contemporary Jewish Religious Thought: Original Essays on Critical Concepts, Movements, and Beliefs*, ed. Arthur Cohen and Paul Mendes-Flohr (New York, 1987), pp. 451–72; and "Who Is an Educated Jew?" *Tel Aviv Review* 2 (1989/90): 177–88.

16. The anecdote in which Steinschneider made his famous remark is retold by Gershom Scholem in his essay on Wissenschaft des Judentums, "The Science of Judaism—Then and Now," trans. Michael A. Meyer and reprinted in *The Messianic Idea in Judaism and Other Essays on Jewish Spirituality* (New York, 1971), p. 307. Steinschneider was, of course, one of the central figures in the Wissenschaft movement at the end of the last century and beginning of this one. On Wissenschaft's ideological dimensions, see Meyer, "The Emergence of Modern Jewish Historiography: Motives and Motifs," *History and Theory* 27 (1988): 160–75; Leon Wieseltier, "*Etwas Uber Die Judische Historik*: Leopold Zunz and the Inception of Modern Jewish Historiography," *History and Theory* 20 (1981): 135–49.

17. David Myers, "The Scholem-Kurzweil Debate and Modern Jewish Historiography," *Modern Judaism* 6 (1986): 277.

18. Yosef Hayim Yerushalmi, *Zakhor: Jewish History and Jewish Memory* (1982; reprint, New York, 1989), p. 81.

19. Ibid., p. 86

20. Ibid.

21. For some observations on other antihistoricizing tendencies in modern Jewish scholarship, see Myers, "Remembering *Zakhor*: A Super-Commentary," *History and Memory* 4 (1992): 129–48.

22. See Barry Holtz, "Midrash and Modernity: Can Midrash Serve a Contemporary Religious Discourse?" in *The Uses of Tradition: Jewish Continuity in the Modern Era*, ed. Jack Wertheimer (New York, 1992), pp. 377–91, esp. pp. 381, 388.

23. Harold Bloom, *The Strong Light of the Canonical* (New York, 1987), p. 77.

24. Ibid. See also Stern, "The Supreme Fictionalist," *The New Republic*, 4 February 1991, pp. 34–40.

25. Bloom, *Kabbalah and Criticism* (New York, 1975).

26. Hartman, "Who Is an Educated Jew?" p. 186.

27. Scholem, "Revelation and Tradition as Religious Categories in Judaism," in *The Messianic Idea in Judaism*, pp. 282–303; *On the Kabbalah and Its Symbolism*, trans. Ralph Manheim (New York, 1969).

28. George Steiner, "The Friend of a Friend," *The New Yorker*, 22 January 1990, p. 133.

Chapter 1

1. Zhang Longxi, *The Tao and the Logos: Literary Hermeneutics, East and West* (Durham, N.C., 1992), p. 24. Note that Derrida does not draw a direct parallel between deconstruction and classical Chinese hermeneutics but between Chinese writing and a nonlogocentric (or nonphonetic) system. What Zhang rightly questions is the degree to which Chinese writing can be said to be nonlogocentric. Derrida himself, with proper caution, does not ascribe to Chinese writing a fully nonphonetic (or, one assumes, nonlogocentric) character, and explicitly states that "phonetic" and "nonphonetic" are never pure qualities as such but opposites in theory alone. See Jacques Derrida, *Of Grammatology*, trans. Gayatri Chakravorty Spivak (Baltimore, 1976), p. 89.

2. See Christopher L. Miller, "Theories of Africans: The Question of Literary Anthropology," *Critical Inquiry* 13 (1986): 120–39.

3. Babylonian Talmud (hereafter B.) Sanhedrin 34a. See also B. Shabbat 88b. Unless otherwise noted, all translations from Talmudic and midrashic texts are my own.

4. For a full exposition of the two exegeses, see David Stern, "Literary Criticism or Literary Homilies? Susan Handelman and the Contemporary Study of Midrash," *Prooftexts* 5 (1985): 102–3 n. 1.

5. Bamidbar Rabbah 13:15; *Mishnat Rabbi Eliezer o Midrash Shloshim u-Shtayim Middot*, ed. H. G. Enelow (New York, 1933), p. 45; *The Alphabet of Rabbi Akiba [Otiot de-Rabbi Akiva]*, in *Batei Midrashot*, ed. S. A. Wertheimer, 2 vols. (Jerusalem, 1968), 2:354; B. Shabbat 88b. For discussion, see W. Bacher, "Seventy-two Modes of Exposition," *Jewish Quarterly Review* o.s. 4 (1892): 509, and Gershom G. Scholem, *On the Kabbalah and Its Symbolism*, trans. Ralph Manheim (New York, 1969), pp. 62–63.

6. B. Hagigah 3a–b.

7. It is worth noting that elsewhere in early Rabbinic literature Exod. 20:1 is given other interpretations suggesting polysemy. Thus, in *Mekhilta de-Rabbi Ishmael*, trans. and ed. Jacob Z. Lauterbach, 3 vols. (Philadelphia, 1933), 2:228, the verse is interpreted to mean that God spoke all ten commandments in a single utterance. See also *Siphre D'Be Rab*, ed. H. S. Horovitz, 2 vols. (Jerusalem, 1966), 1:47–48 and 100.

8. Jerusalem Talmud (hereafter J.) Sanhedrin 4:2, 22a–b; B. Baba Mezi'a 59b. On the latter text, see my discussion below.

9. B. Eruvin 13b.

10. The first statement is found in Mishnah Yebamot 1:4; the exegesis is recorded in the Talmudic discussion in B. Yebamot 14b. Note that according to this tradition the House of Shammai also married the daughters of the other house,

and acted ethically, as did the members of the House of Hillel. In effect, it reads the verses as "you must love *each other* in truth and peace."

11. Geoffrey H. Hartman, *Criticism in the Wilderness* (New Haven, Conn., 1980), p. 270.

12. Ibid., p. 271. But compare Hartman's sensitive comments on irony, specifically in connection with the reading of sacred literature, on pp. 278ff.

13. See A. Leo Oppenheim, "The Interpretation of Dreams in the Ancient Near East," *Transactions of the American Philosophical Society* n.s. 46 (1956): 217–37, and, more recently, Michael Fishbane, *Biblical Interpretation in Ancient Israel* (Oxford, 1985), pp. 443–99.

14. Bacher, *Erkhei Midrash* (Tel Aviv, 1923), pp. 272–74. For the biblical use of *patar* as referring to dream interpretation, see the Joseph story, specifically Gen. 40:8, 22, and numerous other occasions in that chapter and the next one.

15. The classic statement of the connection between Qumranic exegesis and ancient dream interpretation is Lou H. Silberman, "Unriddling the Riddle: A Study in the Structure and Language of the Habakkuk Pesher (1Qp Hab.)," *Révue de Qumran* 3 (1961): 323–64. See also, more recently, Fishbane, "The Qumran Pesher and Traits of Ancient Hermeneutics," in *Proceedings of the Sixth World Congress of Jewish Studies* (Jerusalem, 1977), pp. 97–114.

16. Fishbane, in "The Qumran Pesher and Traits of Ancient Hermeneutics," p. 99, cites Pesher Habakkuk 2:1–10 (in G. Vermes, *The Dead Sea Scrolls in English* [New York, 1975], p. 236) as a case of multiple interpretations, but these examples are actually variants upon a single theme. The same is admittedly true of many examples in Rabbinic midrash.

17. For the classic statement of the connection between ancient dream interpretation and Rabbinic hermeneutics, see Saul Lieberman, *Hellenism in Jewish Palestine*, 2d improved ed. (New York, 1962), pp. 68–82, and, more recently, Jeffrey H. Tigay, "An Early Technique of Aggadic Exegesis," in *History, Historiography, and Interpretation: Studies in Biblical and Cuneiform Literatures*, ed. H. Tadmor and M. Weinfeld (Jerusalem, 1983), pp. 169–89. Lieberman cites the famous passage attached to the thirty-two hermeneutical methods of aggadah: " 'Behold it says: *"A dream carries much implication"* (Eccl. 5:2). Now by using the method of *kal vehomer (a minori ad maius)* we reason: If the contents of dreams which have no effect may yield a multitude of interpretations, how much more then should the important concerns of the Torah imply many interpretations in every verse' " (p. 70). While this text suggests that a dream may have more than one interpretation, ancient dream interpretation seems to assume in general that a dream has only a single correct interpretation (although it is quite obvious that a symbol or figure may have different meanings in different dreams). One should recall as well that this passage is a late text, probably from the Geonic period in the ninth–tenth centuries, and that it very possibly was written in response to Karaite polemics in order to rationalize Rabbinic hermeneutics.

The major classical source for Rabbinic dream interpretation is the lengthy section in B. Berakhot 55a–57b; note the statement in 55b attributed to Rabbi Bana'ah: "There were twenty-four interpreters of dreams in Jerusalem. Once I dreamt a dream and I went round to all of them and they all gave different interpretations and all were fulfilled, thus confirming that which is said: All dreams follow the mouth [of the interpreter]." Note, too, the lengthy section in 56a illustrating the latter tradition that "all dreams follow the mouth": Abbaye and Raba each consult the dream interpreter Bar Hedya about the meaning of the same dream; however, Abbaye pays Bar Hedya for his interpretation, Raba does not, and Bar Hedya consistently gives the one who pays him a favorable interpretation and the one who does not an unfavorable reading. While these passages suggest that the same dream may have more than one meaning, it should be noted that: (1) the text does not confirm that both interpretations were fulfilled; (2) the passage as a whole seems to be a mocking polemic against professional dream interpreters like Bar Hedya rather than a serious statement about dream interpretation; and (3) the Talmud nowhere states that both interpretations were correct or that they were both fulfilled. Moreover, ancient dream interpretation seemed to assume that correct interpretation was dependent upon knowledge of the nature of the dreamer, not just the dream; the same dream could have different meanings for good and bad people. See Daldianus Artemidorus, *The Interpretation of Dreams*, trans. Robert J. White (Park Ridge, N.J., 1975), where Artemidorus explicitly states that it is impossible for different elements in a dream to contradict each other, that is, for the same image to be both good and bad, "if dreams are to foretell occurences that will inevitably take place" (p. 175). See also the discussion of Artemidorus in Michel Foucault, *The Care of the Self*, vol. 3 of *The History of Sexuality*, trans. Robert Hurley (New York, 1986), pp. 4–36.

18. For an example of a petirah of this sort, see Vayikra Rabbah 10:1–3.

19. On this question, see, in particular, James A. Coulter, *The Literary Microcosm: Theories of Interpretation of the Later Neoplatonists* (Leiden, 1976), pp. 67, 87–89. As Coulter argues, the credit for devising the theory of ascending levels of meaning, all related analogically in a unified structure, should probably go to Iamblichus. See also Jean Pépin, "Remarques sur la théorie de l'exégèse allégorique chez Philon," in *Philon d'Alexandrie*, ed. Roger Arnaldez, Claude Mondésert, and Jean Poupilloux (Paris, 1967), pp. 131–67; Philip Rollinson, *Classical Theories of Allegory and Christian Culture* (Pittsburgh, 1981); H. A. Wolfson, *Philo: Foundations of Religious Philosophy in Judaism, Christianity, and Islam*, 2 vols. (Cambridge, Mass., 1948), 1:87–163; and, on early medieval exegesis, Beryl Smalley, *The Study of the Bible in the Middle Ages* (Notre Dame, Ind., 1970).

20. Augustine, *The Confessions of St. Augustine*, trans. and ed. John K. Ryan (Garden City, N.Y., 1960), p. 360. On the history of the interpretation of this verse, including Augustine's allegorization, see Jeremy Cohen's comprehensive study, "*Be*

Fertile and Increase, Fill the Earth and Master It": The Ancient and Medieval Career of a Biblical Text (Ithaca, N.Y., 1989).

21. Augustine, *The Confessions*, p. 321.

22. Augustine, *On Christian Doctrine*, trans. D. W. Robertson (Indianapolis, 1958), p. 102. See, too, Robertson's remarks in his introduction, pp. xi–xii and xiv–xvi.

23. Ibid., p. 31.

24. Max Kadushin, "The Indeterminacy of Belief," *Conservative Judaism* 33 (1980): 3–6, and *The Rabbinic Mind* (New York, 1952). A similar (and among students of midrash, more famous) model for midrashic discourse, framed in romanticist language and virtually Viconian mythopoeiac terminology, was proposed by Yitzhak Heinemann in his classic *Darkhei ha'aggadah [The Methods of Aggadah]*, 3d ed. (Jerusalem, 1970).

25. Frank Kermode, *The Art of Telling: Essays on Fiction* (Cambridge, Mass., 1983), p. 171.

26. For an attempt to sketch the history of this editorial tendency and its academic motivations, see David Weiss Halivni, *Midrash, Mishnah, and Gemara: The Jewish Predilection for Justified Law* (Cambridge, 1986), pp. 108–11. For examples of one Rabbi dismissing and condemning the interpretations of another Rabbi, see the famous passage in B. Sanhedrin 67b (in which Rabbi Eleazar ben Azariah attacked Rabbi Akiba for interpreting Exod. 8:2, "And the frog [singular] came up and covered the land of Egypt," as meaning that "there was only one frog and it filled the whole land of Egypt"); *Sifre Deuteronomy*, ed. L. Finkelstein (1939; reprint, New York, 1969), p. 7, and Finkelstein's note ad loc.; Vayikra Rabbah 5:1.

27. Compare, however, the remarks of Morton Smith, "The Image of God: Notes on the Hellenization of Judaism, with Especial Reference to Goodenough's Work on Jewish Symbols," *Bulletin of the John Rylands Library* 40 (1957–58): 473–481 and 487ff. The scholarly debate over internal censorship revolves largely around the arguments of Erwin Goodenough in *Jewish Symbols in the Greco-Roman Period*, 13 vols. (New York, 1953–68).

28. See Raphael Loewe, "The 'Plain' Meaning of Scripture in Early Jewish Exegesis," *Papers of the Institute of Jewish Studies* 1 (1964): 140–85, and, more recently, W. Sibley Towner, "Hermeneutical Systems of Hillel and the Tannaim: A Fresh Look," *Hebrew Union College Annual* 53 (1982): 101–35, a clear but slightly outdated presentation.

29. Betty Roitman, "Sacred Language and Open Text," in *Midrash and Literature*, ed. Geoffrey H. Hartman and Sanford Budick (New Haven, Conn., 1986), p. 160. Akiba's saying is found in Mishnah Avot 3:19.

30. J. Peah 17a.

31. *Pesikta de-Rab Kahana*, ed. B. Mandelbaum, 2 vols. (New York, 1963), 1:223; see also Shemot Rabbah 3:6.

32. *Midrash Bereshit Rabbah*, ed. J. Theodor and Ch. Albeck, 3 vols., 2d ed. (Jerusalem, 1965), 1:1–2.

33. For examples of the law as education/teacher motif in Patristic literature, see Stephen D. Benin, "Sacrifice as Education in Augustine and Chrysostom," *Church History* 52 (1983): 7–20. For the image of the architect, see Iranaeus of Lyon, *Adversus Haereses*, ed. W. W. Harvey (Cambridge, 1857), 4.25.2, 3. In our midrashic passage, the Rabbis seem to be arguing that the law was devised not as a form of accomodation to the historical nature of the Jewish people but that it was a condition of the universe's existence.

34. See Ephraim E. Urbach, *The Sages: Their Concepts and Beliefs*, trans. Israel Abrahams, 2 vols. (Jerusalem, 1975), 1:199–201, who argues against a connection between the Platonic Logos and Rabbi Hoshaya's image. For an interesting attempt to argue the connection, however, see David Winston, *Logos and Mystical Theology in Philo of Alexandria* (Cincinnati, 1985), p. 25 and passim.

35. *Sifre Deuteronomy* 49, p. 115; Judah Goldin, "The Freedom and Restraint of Haggadah," in *Midrash and Literature*, pp. 57–76.

36. Moshe Idel, "Infinities of Torah in Kabbalah," in *Midrash and Literature*, pp. 151–52.

37. For these sources, see Idel, "The Concept of Torah in the Heikhalot and the Kabbalah" [Hebrew], in *Jerusalem Studies in Jewish Thought* 1 (1981), esp. pp. 42–46. See also Gershom Scholem, "The Name of God and the Linguistic Theory of Kabbalah," *Diogenes*, nos. 79–80 (1972): 68–80, 164–94.

38. Idel, "Infinities of Torah in Kabbalah," p. 144.

39. Note, for example, Vayikra Rabbah 16:4; for discussion, see David Halperin, *The Merkabah in Rabbinic Literature* (New Haven, Conn., 1980), pp. 128–33, and bibliography cited there.

40. B. Baba Mezi'a 59a–b.

41. Joseph Blenkinsopp, "Interpretation and the Tendency to Sectarianism: An Aspect of Second Temple History," in *Jewish and Christian Self-Definition*, ed. E. P. Sanders et al., 3 vols. (Philadelphia, 1981), 2:1–26.

42. Pesher Habakkuk 7 (in Vermes, *The Dead Sea Scrolls in English*, p. 239).

43. Koheleth Rabbah 2:16; see Mishnah Avot 6:6, and *Midrasch Tanhuma*, ed. Salomon Buber, 2 vols. (Wilna, 1885; reprint, Jerusalem, 1964), 2: Numbers 11a–b.

44. For a recent collection of articles on such redactional models, see *Empirical Models for Biblical Criticism*, ed. Jeffrey H. Tigay (Philadelphia, 1985).

45. Pliny, *Naturalis Historia* 2.5.

46. For the most recent bibliography on this subject, see Lee Levine, *The Rabbinic Class of Roman Palestine in Late Antiquity* (Jerusalem and New York, 1989), esp. pp. 83–97; Robert Goldenberg, "History and Ideology in Talmudic Narrative," in *Approaches to Ancient Judaism*, ed. William Scott Green, 5 vols. (Chico, Calif., 1983), 4:159–71; David Goodblatt, "The Story of the Plot against R. Simeon

b. Gamliel II," *Zion* 49 (1984): 349–74; A. Baumgarten, "Rabbi Judah and His Opponents, *Journal of Jewish Studies* 12 (1981): 135–72; Baumgarten, "The Akiban Opposition," *Hebrew Union College Annual* 50 (1980): 179–97. See also the interesting philosophical reading of Berakhot 27b–28a by Menahem Fisch, "Ecclesiastes (Qohelet) in Context—A Study of Wisdom as Constructive Skepticism," in *Critical Rationalism: Essays for Joseph Agassi*, ed. I. C. Jarvie and Nathaniel Laor, 2 vols. (Dordrecht, 1995), pp. 167–87.

47. The story is recounted in several places in the Talmud: B. Berakhot 27b–28a; J. Berakhot 7c–d; J. Taanit 67d.

48. Rashi ad loc.

49. For a comprehensive study of the passage and its parallels elsewhere in Rabbinic literature, see Shragga Abramson, "Four Topics in Midrash Halakha" [Hebrew], *Sinai* 74 (1973): 1–7.

50. It is worth noting that the interpretations of Deut. 26:17–18 are based on two words, *heemarta* and *heemirkha*, which together constitute a *hapax legomenon*. The classical Talmudic commentators suggest different meanings to characterize the uniqueness of the proclamations God and Israel make to each other. For an additional suggestion as to the meanings of these words, see Judah Goldin, *The Song at the Sea: Being a Commentary on a Commentary in Two Parts* (New Haven, Conn., 1971), p. 109; Goldin connects the words to the name of a special kind of hem on a distinctive article of clothing (like, perhaps, the fringes on the prayer shawl or *talit?*).

51. For reasons I do not understand, Rashi attributes the third homily to Rabbi Joshua, not Rabbi Eleazar; he does not explain, however, how the closing statement of Rabbi Joshua praising Rabbi Eleazar is then to be read.

52. B. Berakhot 27b.

53. See Edward W. Said, *The World, the Text, and the Critic* (Cambridge, Mass., 1983), pp. 31–53.

Chapter 2

1. Vayikra Rabbah 28:2. I have translated the text from the critical edition of Vayikra Rabbah, *Midrash Wayyikra Rabbah*, ed. Mordecai Margoulies, 3 vols. (Jerusalem, 1972), 2:653–55. For parallels, see Margoulies's notes ad loc., and esp. Koheleth Rabbah 1:3.1. My discussion of this passage, as well as much of the rest of this chapter, draws on the far fuller treatment of the Rabbinic mashal in my book *Parables in Midrash: Narrative and Exegesis in Rabbinic Literature* (Cambridge, Mass., 1991).

2. On Rabbinic fables, see, most recently, Aharon Singer's "A Study of Fox Fables in Rabbinic Literature" [Hebrew], *Jerusalem Studies in Jewish Folklore* 4 (1983):

79–91, and bibliography cited there. Note as well that the use of three hundred for the number of fox fables Bar Kappara tells is conventional. Compare the fox fable in Bereshit Rabbah 78:7 in which the protagonist, a fox, himself recites three hundred fox fables!

3. Note that the Ecclesiasteslike proverb Bar Kappara writes on Rabbi Shimeon's door is also called a mashal. Compare the version of the narrative in B. Nedarim 3b.

4. See Bereshit Rabbah 64:9; B. Berakhot 61b.

5. See Mekhilta (Bahodesh 6); B. Avodah Zarah 11a and 54b–55a; B. Rosh Hashana 17b; and B. Sanhedrin 91a.

6. For the mashal as an instrument of social politesse: B. Baba Kama 60b and 66b; J. Taanit 4.5, 66c–d; B. Taanit 5b; compare the story of Rabbi Kahana in J. Berakhot 5c. For eulogies: Abot deRabbi Natan A, 14.6; J. Berakhot 5b–c.

7. Semahot deRabbi Hiyya 4.1.

8. See, however, the mashal of Rabbi Akiba in B. Nidah 45a, and B. Berakhot 11a for the mashal used in the argument between Rabbi Ishmael and Rabbi Eleazar ben Azariah.

9. This is an approximate number based upon the meshalim collected by I. Ziegler in his monumental anthology *Die Konigsgleichnisse des Midrasch* (Breslau, 1903), and by Robert Johnston in his dissertation, "Parabolic Interpretations Attributed to Tannaim," The Hartford Seminary Foundation, 1978.

10. Shir Hashirim Rabbah 1:8.

11. Ibid.

12. On ideological narrative, see Susan Rubin Suleiman, *Authoritarian Fictions: The Ideological Novel as a Literary Genre* (New York, 1983).

13. See W. S. Kissinger, *The Parables of Jesus: A History of Interpretation and Bibliography* (Metuchen, N.J., 1979). Compare my critique of more contemporary New Testament scholarship in "Jesus' Parables from the Perspective of Rabbinic Literature: The Example of the Wicked Husbandmen," in *Parable and Story in Judaism and Christianity*, ed. Clemens Thoma and Michael Wyschogrod (New York, 1989), pp. 42–80.

14. For the use of this model in earlier scholarship about the mashal, see Ziegler, *Die Konigsgleichnisse des Midrasch*, and Tovia Gutmann, *Hamashal Bitekufat Hatannaim* (Jerusalem, 1949).

15. A striking example is in Bereshit Rabbah 1:1, which portrays God as creator through a description of an architect who builds a palace using a blueprint and an illustration (which symbolize the Torah). In this case, the mashal is also about illustration!

16. For an example, see *Tanna de-Bei Eliyahu* 18:8. This use of the mashal ties in closely with the overall homiletical thrust of the work. For one example in Maimonides, see the Parable of the Palace in *Guide of the Perplexed*, pt. 3, chap. 51.

17. Frank Kermode, *The Genesis of Secrecy: On the Interpretation of Narrative* (Cambridge, 1979), esp. pp. 23–47.

18. See J. Bowker, "Mystery and Parable: Mark 4, 1–20," *Journal of Theological Studies* n.s. 25 (1974): 300–317.

19. For this view, see David Daube, *Ancient Hebrew Fables* (Oxford, 1973), and *The New Testament and Rabbinic Judaism* (New York, 1973), pp. 141–50.

20. *Midrasch Tanhuma,* ed. Salomon Buber, 2 vols. (Wilna, 1885; reprint, Jerusalem, 1964), 1: Genesis, 103.

21. For an additional example, see *Midrash Debarim Rabbah* 8:5, ed. Saul Lieberman (Jerusalem, 1974), p. 110.

22. For examples, see Sefer Habahir 33 (and compare its Rabbinic model, Eikhah Rabbah 2:1) and *Sefer HaZohar,* ed. Reuven Margaliot, 3 vols., 6th ed. (Jerusalem, 1984), 2:99a–b.

23. The definition I have offered is based on W. J. Verdenius, "AINOS," *Mnemosyne* 15 (1962): 389. See also Gregory Nagy, *The Best of the Achaeans: Concepts of the Hero in Archaic Greek Poetry* (Baltimore, 1979), pp. 239, 280–90.

24. Lieberman, notes to *Midrash Wayyikra Rabbah,* 2:870. Margoulies himself differs; he defines the *ma'aforet* as a special kind of turban or headdress.

25. See, for example, the other mashal in Vayikra Rabbah 2:5, and the remainder of the chapter.

26. Such implied comparative techniques are so common they are virtual conventions of the polemic genre. The most frequent forms are comparisons between two people or things to see who is the most precious (*haviv*), as in Bereshit Rabbah 30:10 (which compares Abraham and Noah); or the comparison between the one and the many, as in *Midrasch Tanhuma,* 2: Leviticus, 78; or between one person and everyone else, as in Eikhah Rabbah 3:24.

27. For apologetic praise, Eikhah Rabbah 4:11; apologetic blame, Midrash Tehillim, p. 485; for polemic, Bereshit Rabbah 1:12, and most meshalim that begin "It is the custom of the world," whose purpose is to condemn the pretensions to divinity of the imperial cult; for lament, the parables in notes 6 and 7 above, as well as *Midrasch Tanhuma,* 2: Deuteronomy, 13; for complaint, Eikhah Rabbah 1:21 and 3:1; for regret, Bereshit Rabbah 5:1; for warning, *Sifre Deuteronomy* 48.

28. The text translated here is that of the Ashkenazic recension of Eikhah Rabbah; for the Hebrew, see the critical text I prepared in *Parables in Midrash*, pp. 281–82. Buber's text in his edition, *Midrasch Echa Rabbati* (Wilna, 1899), p. 132, is closest to the Ashkenazic recension, while the text in the Wilna folio edition of Midrash Rabbah, p. 26a, is closer to the Sephardic recension (in *Parables in Midrash*, p. 283).

29. Note, however, that the *ketubah* in the mashal is more like the Biblical *mohar* or dowry than the Rabbinic *ketubah*. See Mordechai A. Friedman, *Jewish Marriage in Palestine. A Cairo Geniza Study*, 2 vols. (Tel Aviv and New York, 1980–81), 1:77,

239–62. In addition to the conventional symbols, note that the various motifs used in the mashal are nearly all traditional. See my comments on stereotyping below; on this particular mashal, see my Hebrew article, a much earlier version of this chapter, "The Function of the Parable in Rabbinic Literature," *Jerusalem Studies in Hebrew Literature* 7 (1985): 99 n. 33, for discussion of specific parallels.

30. *Digest* 50.17.30, 24.1.32.13; Ulpian, cited and discussed in Susan Treggiari, "Roman Marriage," in *Civilization of the Ancient Mediterranean: Greece and Rome*, ed. Michael Grant and Rachel Kitzinger, 3 vols. (New York, 1988), 3:1345.

31. For more on the interpretation of *zot*, see especially Yitzhak Heinemann, *Darkhei ha'aggadah*, 3d ed. (Jerusalem, 1970), p. 118.

32. Alan Mintz, *Hurban* (New York, 1984), pp. 34ff.

33. I wish to thank Professor Michael Sokoloff for pointing this out to me.

34. In the Sephardic recension, this leap into the future is even more explicit: the verb following *lemahar*, *kesheyavo*, is also in the future tense.

35. Stern, *Parables in Midrash*, pp. 21–37.

36. Erich Auerbach, *Mimesis: The Representation of Reality in Western Literature*, trans. Willard R. Trask (Princeton, N.J., 1953). The phrase Auerbach actually uses to describe the biblical mode of representation is "fraught with background" (p. 12), but see more generally pp. 7–16.

37. On gaps generally, see in particular Meir Sternberg, *The Poetics of Biblical Narrative: Ideological Literature and the Drama of Reading* (Bloomington, Ind., 1985), esp. pp. 186–263. On the mashal in particular, see Stern, *Parables in Midrash*, pp. 74–82.

38. The terms quoted are taken from Gerald Prince, "Introduction to the Study of the Narratee," in *Reader-Response Criticism: From Formalism to Post-Structuralism*, ed. Jane P. Tompkins (Baltimore, 1980), pp. 7–25; Wolfgang Iser, *The Implied Reader: Patterns of Communication in Prose Fiction from Bunyan to Beckett* (Baltimore, 1974); Naomi Schor, "Fiction as Interpretation/Interpretation as Fiction," in *The Reader in the Text: Essays on Audience and Interpretation*, ed. Susan R. Suleiman and Inge Crosman (Princeton, N.J., 1980), pp. 165–82.

39. Iser, *The Implied Reader*, p. 55, and esp. chap. 5, "The Reader as a Component Part of the Realistic Novel," pp. 101–20.

40. *Kal vehomer* is an argument *ad minori ad maius* (from the lighter or less significant to the heavier or more significant); *notarikon* (from the Latin *notarius*, stenographer) is a kind of interpretation that reads Scriptural words as though they were shorthand or abbreviations for lengthier words or phrases; *gematriyah* is a form of *notarikon* that dwells on numerical equivalencies. All of these interpretive techniques are examples of the traditional *middot*, the so-called hermeneutical principles of midrash. For full discussion and background, see H. L. Strack and G. Stemberger, *Introduction to the Talmud and Midrash*, trans. Markus Bockmuehl (Minneapolis, 1992), pp. 17–34.

41. See Jonathan Culler, "Literary Competence," in *Structuralist Poetics: Structuralism, Linguistics and the Study of Literature* (Ithaca, N.Y., 1975), pp. 113–30.

Chapter 3

1. For some discussion of these questions, see Yonah Fraenkel, *Darkhei Haaggadah Vehamidrash*, 2 vols. (Jerusalem, 1991), 1:16–43; Marc Hirshman, "The Preacher and His Public," *Journal of Jewish Studies* 42 (1991): 108–14; Jacob Neusner, *Judaism and Scripture: The Evidence of Leviticus Rabbah* (Chicago, 1986); Neusner, *Comparative Midrash: The Plan and Program of Genesis and Leviticus Rabbah* (Atlanta, 1986); Steven D. Fraade, "Interpreting Midrash 1: Midrash and the History of Judaism," *Prooftexts* 7 (1987): 178–94; Hirshman, "The Greek Fathers and the Aggada on Ecclesiastes: Formats of Exegesis in Late Antiquity," *Hebrew Union College Annual* 59 (1988): 138–65.

2. All references are to *Midrash Wayyikra Rabbah*, ed. Mordecai Margoulies, 3 vols. (Jerusalem, 1972), 1:1–32. An English translation of the chapter, along with the entire midrash, may be found in the Soncino series, in *Midrash Rabbah: Leviticus*, trans. J. Israelstam (London, 1939), pp. 1–17 (note that para. 15 on pp. 17–18 is not an authentic part of the text according to Margoulies). The Soncino translation is based on an uncritical text; all translations in this chapter are my own.

3. This, admittedly, is something of an exaggeration since redactional organization can be discerned in sections of the *Mekhilta* (Shirta especially), Bereshit Rabbah, and Eikhah Rabbah. The distinction between the two genres of midrash is partly heuristic; still, there is no consistent or systematic plan to the exegetical anthology.

4. On the triennial cycle and its relation to the homiletical midrash, see Jacob Mann, *The Bible as Read and Preached in the Old Synagogue*, ed. I. Sonne, 2 vols. (Cincinnati, 1940–66); J. Heinemann, "The Triennial Lectionary Cycle," *Journal of Jewish Studies* 19 (1968): 41–48; M. Bregman, "The Triennial Haftarot and the Perorations of the Midrashic Homilies," *Journal of Jewish Studies* 32 (1981): 74–84.

5. For example, see J. Theodor, "Zur Composition der aggadischen Homilien," *Monatsschrift für Geschichte und Wissenschaft des Judentums* 29 (1879): 108; Chanoch Albeck, "Midrash Leviticus Rabbah," in *Louis Ginzberg Jubilee Volume*, ed. Alexander Marx (New York, 1946), Hebrew section, pp. 25ff.; Margoulies, introduction to *Midrash Wayyikra Rabbah*, 3.5:ix–x.

6. J. Heinemann, "The Art of Composition in Midrash Leviticus Rabbah" [Hebrew], *Hasifrut* 2 (1971): 808–34, published in a shortened English version as "Profile of a Midrash," *Journal of the American Academy of Religion* 39 (1971): 141–50; see also Heinemann, *Public Sermons in the Talmudic Period* [Hebrew] (Jerusalem, 1970), and "Sections of Leviticus Rabbah Whose Originality Is Questionable" [Hebrew], *Tarbiz* 37 (1967–68): 339–54. Heinemann's influence upon other scholars who have written about the homily has been considerable. See, for example, L. H. Silberman, "Toward a Rhetoric of Midrash: A Preliminary Account," in *The Biblical Mosaic: Changing Perspectives*, ed. Robert Polzin and Eugene Rothman (Philadelphia,

1982), pp. 15–26, and "A Theological Treatise on Forgiveness: Chapter Twenty-Three of Pesiqta Derab Kahana," in *Studies in Aggadah, Targum, and Jewish Liturgy in Memory of Joseph Heinemann*, ed. J. Petuchowski and E. Fleischer (Jerusalem, 1981), pp. 95–107; L. M. Barth, "Literary Imagination and the Rabbinic Sermon," in *Proceedings of the Seventh World Congress of Jewish Studies* (Jerusalem, 1981), pp. 29–36.

7. The notion of organic unity poses both literary-theoretical problems and practical-midrashic ones. On the former, see R. Scholes and R. Kellogg, *The Nature of Narrative* (New York, 1976), pp. 106–7; on the latter, see N. J. Cohen, "Scripture and Editing in the Homiletic Midrashim," *AJS Review* 6 (1981): 1–20.

8. Heinemann, "The Proem in Aggadic Midrashim: A Form-Critical Study," *Scripta Hierosolymitana* 22 (1971): 100–122; Heinemann, "The Petihtaot of the Aggadic Midrash—Their Origin and Function" [Hebrew], in *Proceedings of the Fourth World Congress of Jewish Studies* (Jerusalem, 1965), pp. 43–47; earlier bibliography is cited in the notes of both articles. In addition, see Heinemann's interpretive articles, "The Amoraim of Israel as Artists of the Sermon" [Hebrew], *Hasifrut* 25 (1977): 808–34, and "On Life and Death: Anatomy of a Rabbinic Sermon," *Scripta Hierosolymitana* 27 (1978): 52–65. See also A. M. Goldberg, "Petihta und Hariza," *Journal for the Study of Judaism* 10 (1980): 213–18; Avigdor Shinan, "On the Petihta" [Hebrew], *Jerusalem Studies in Hebrew Literature* 1 (1981): 135–42; Bregman, "Circular Proems and Proems Beginning with the Formula *Zo hi shene'emra beruah hakodesh*" [Hebrew], in *Studies in Aggadah, Targum, and Jewish Liturgy*, 34–51; R. S. Sarason, "The Petihtaot in Leviticus Rabbah: 'Oral Homilies' or Redactional Constructions?" *Journal of Jewish Studies* 33 (1982): 557–67; and, most recently, M. S. Jaffee, "The 'Midrashic' Proem: Towards the Description of Rabbinic Exegesis," in *Approaches to Ancient Judaism*, ed. William Scott Green, 5 vols. (Chico, Calif., 1983), 4:95–112.

9. On the attribution, see Margoulies's note in *Midrash Wayyikra Rabbah*, 1:1, where he explicitly describes the petihta as a redactional construction.

10. The redactor's desire to create more subjects than the verse itself warrants is proved by the fact that the proof phrase for section C, "ye . . . that fulfill His word, hearkening," overlaps with the preceding and subsequent proof phrase (B and D).

11. On atomization, see I. Heinemann, *The Methods of Aggadah* [Hebrew] (Jerusalem, 1970), pp. 96ff.

12. See S. Safrai, "The Observance of the Sabbatical Year Following the Destruction of the Second Temple" [Hebrew], *Tarbiz* 35 (1966): 304–28; 36 (1967): 1–21, esp. p. 15. Note that Margoulies (*Midrash Wayyikra Rabbah*, 1:4) rejects Safrai's reading of *arnona*, the special tax the Romans levied upon the Jews, in favor of *annona*; but see Saul Lieberman's correction in *Midrash Wayyikra Rabbah*, 2:869.

13. On the peroration, see E. Stein, "Die homiletische Peroratio im Midrash," *Hebrew Union College Annual* 8–9 (1931–32): 353–71, and Bregman, "The Triennial Haftarot and the Perorations of the Midrashic Homilies."

14. On the reading *otanin,* not *ikonin,* see Margoulies's note in *Midrash Wayyikra Rabbah,* 1:32; but for the correct interpretation of the Greek loanword *othanion*, see Lieberman's note in ibid., 2:870.

15. On the conversion of Bityah and her rejection of idolatry, see Shemot Rabbah 1:23; see also Targum Yerushalmi ad Exod. 2:5.

16. See B. Megillah 13a, and Margoulies's note in *Midrash Wayyikra Rabbah,* 1:7–8.

17. See *The Interpreter's Bible,* ed. G. A. Buttrick, 12 vols. (New York, 1951–57), 2:528–29; *Mikra'ot Gedolot* and commentaries ad loc.; for a different interpretation of the word, see Nahmanides ad loc.

18. *Sifre Deuteronomy,* ed. L. Finkelstein (1939; reprint, New York, 1969), 400–401.

19. See, however, para. 13, where God's speech to Jewish prophets is contrasted with His speech to Gentiles. To the latter, he speaks in the language of impurity; to the former, "in the language of holiness, the language of purity, a clear language, the language in which the angelic host praise Him." In his apparatus, Margoulies quotes variants that correspond to the versions of the lemma in Bereshit Rabbah 52:5 and 74:7 (cited in *Midrash Bereshit Rabbah,* ed. J. Theodor and Ch. Albeck, 3 vols., 2d ed. [Jerusalem, 1965], 2:544, 864), which read, respectively, *leshon hibah* (the language of love) and *leshon kedushah vehibah* (the language of holiness and love). Here, again, one notes the antiphonal character of language, which we saw in the first petihta.

20. On praise in the parable, see David Stern, *Parables in Midrash: Narrative and Exegesis in Rabbinic Literature* (Cambridge, Mass., 1991), pp. 51–56.

21. The use of this verse in our homily remains somewhat problematic; see MaHaRZU's comments in the Wilna edition of Midrash Rabbah ad loc.

22. I wish to thank Professor Dov Noy for pointing out this wordplay. See the use of Prov. 20:15 (*ukli yakar siftei da'at*) as the petihta verse in para. 6.

23. Paul Ricoeur, *Interpretation Theory: Discourse and the Surplus of Meaning* (Fort Worth, 1976), pp. 92, 44. See also Jaffee, "The 'Midrashic' Proem," p. 105.

24. E. E. Urbach, "Rabbinic Homilies on Gentile Prophets and on the Biblical Portions Concerning Balaam" [Hebrew], *Tarbiz* 25 (1956): 272–89.

25. On the formula, see M. Hirshman, "The Prophecy of King Solomon and *Ruah ha-kodesh* in Midrash Ecclesiastes Rabbah" [Hebrew], *Jerusalem Studies in Jewish Thought* 3 (1982): 7–14, esp. pp. 12–13.

26. On the origin of the phrase and the application to Augustine and other early Christian writers, see Erich Auerbach, "Sermo Humilis," in *Literary Language and Its Public in Late Latin Antiquity and in the Middle Ages*, trans. R. Manheim (1958; reprint, New York, 1965), pp. 25–81, esp. pp. 45ff. See also Peter Brown, *Augustine of Hippo: A Biography* (London, 1967), pp. 257–58, esp. p. 259.

Chapter 4

1. For a short history of anthropomorphism, Louis Ginzberg's article "Anthropomorphism" in *The Jewish Encyclopaedia*, 12 vols. (New York and London, 1901), 1:621–25, still remains the best single survey. For a recent treatment of the Rabbinic phenomenon within the larger history, see Alon Goshen Gottstein, "The Body as Image of God in Rabbinic Literature," *Harvard Theological Review* 87 (1994): 171–95.

2. Ginzberg, "Anthropomorphism," 1:622. Compare, for our present discussion, James Barr's cautious and wise assessment of the biblical phenomenon in "Theophany and Anthropomorphism in the Old Testament," *Supplements to Vetus Testamentum* 7 (1960): 31–38. Note, in particular, Barr's comments on theophany in human shape: "The most important question which remains is perhaps better phrased thus: not 'Is God conceived of as essentially in human form?', but 'When he does appear in a form at all, is it thought that the human form is the natural or characteristic one for him to assume?' " (p. 33). Worth remembering is Harold Bloom's remark that if we were trees, our God would be dendromorphic; see *The Book of J*, trans. David Rosenberg, interp. Bloom (New York, 1990), p. 282.

3. For God pointing, see Mekhilta Pisha 2; for God swearing, Eikhah Rabbah 2:3; for greeting the fact of God's presence (*lekabeil* or *lehakbil pnei hashekhinah*), B. Sanhedrin 42a.

4. B. Berakhot 6a, 7a.

5. Ignaz Ziegler, *Die Konigsgleichnisse des Midrasch* (Breslau, 1903); David Stern, *Parables in Midrash: Narrative and Exegesis in Rabbinic Literature* (Cambridge, Mass., 1991), esp. pp. 97–101.

6. B. Berakhot 3a, 59a; B. Baba Mezi'a 59b.

7. On this passage and its parallel in *Pesikta deRav Kahana*, Parah 4, see Michael Fishbane, "Some Forms of Divine Appearance in Ancient Jewish Thought," in *From Ancient Israel to Modern Judaism: Intellect in Quest of Understanding*, ed. Jacob Neusner, Ernest S. Frerichs, and Nahum M. Sarna, 4 vols. (Atlanta, 1989), 2:261–70.

8. Mekhilta Bahodesh 4, cited in *Mekhilta de-Rabbi Ishmael*, trans. and ed. Jacob Z. Lauterbach, 3 vols. (Philadelphia, 1933), 2:221. On the phrase *leshabeir et haozen*, see Henoch Yalon, *Pirkei Lashon* (Jerusalem, 1971), pp. 304–7, who lists all the textual variants.

9. See, however, Ginzberg, "Anthropomorphism," who cites Bereshit Rabbah 27:1; Arthur Marmorstein, *The Old Rabbinic Doctrine of God, II. Essays in Anthropomorphism* (1937; reprint, New York, 1968), passim; and my comments below. The phrase *kiveyakhol* is sometimes cited as an instance of ambivalence about anthropomorphism, but see Fishbane's discussion in *The Garments of Torah: Essays in Biblical Hermeneutics* (Bloomington, Ind., 1989), pp. 19–32. The texts in which opposition to anthropomorphism has most often been located in past scholarship are the Targumim, but Michael Klein, in *Anthropomorphisms and Anthropopathisms in*

the Targumim of the Pentateuch (Jerusalem, 1982), effectively destroys the traditional case. See Moshe B. Bernstein's review of Klein's book in *Jewish Quarterly Review* 77 (1986): 65–70.

10. On this, see Ginzberg, "Anthropomorphism," 1:624; Harry A. Wolfson, "Maimonides on Negative Attributes," in *Studies in the History of Philosophy and Religion*, ed. Isadore Twersky and George H. Williams, 2 vols. (Cambridge, Mass., 1973–77), 1:195–230; Josef Stern, "Language," in *Contemporary Jewish Religious Thought: Original Essays on Critical Concepts, Movements and Beliefs*, ed. Arthur A. Cohen and Paul Mendes-Flohr (New York, 1986), pp. 543–51; Josef Stern, "Logical Syntax as a Key to the Secret of the Guide of the Perplexed," *Iyyun* 38 (1989): 136–66. I also wish to thank Josef Stern for helping to clarify the philosophers' position.

11. Saadia Gaon, *The Book of Beliefs and Opinions*, trans. Samuel Rosenblatt (New Haven, Conn., 1946), p. 118.

12. An important exception in this regard is Max Kadushin, whose criticism of the philosophical position closely resembles mine; see his important discussions in *The Rabbinic Mind* (New York, 1972), esp. pp. 273–367. Our approaches to the question of how to deal *non*philosophically with anthropomorphism differ significantly, however; for Kadushin's "normative mysticism," see ibid., pp. 194–272.

13. Marmorstein, *The Old Rabbinic Doctrine of God*, p. 35.

14. Ibid., p. 56.

15. H. A. Wolfson, *Philo: Foundations of Religious Philosophy in Judaism, Christianity, and Islam*, 2 vols., rev. ed. (Cambridge, Mass., 1968), 2:127.

16. Isaac Heinemann, *Darkhei ha'aggadah*, 3d ed. (Jerusalem, 1970), pp. 83–86.

17. Jacob Neusner, *The Incarnation of God: The Character of Divinity in Formative Judaism* (Philadelphia, 1988).

18. See Elliot R. Wolfson's review of Neusner's book in *Jewish Quarterly Review* 81 (1990): 219–21. One must acknowledge, however, that the attempt Neusner makes to trace the development of representations of God through the history of Rabbinic literature is an admirable project; alas, because of the shortcomings in Neusner's treatment, the project remains a desideratum. My own approach in this essay is, admittedly, synchronic rather than diachronic.

19. Neusner, *The Incarnation of God*, p. 171.

20. For evidence and brilliant discussion, see Robin Lane Fox, *Pagans and Christians* (New York, 1987), pp. 102–67.

21. On Gnostic and putative Rabbinic traditions, see Gedaliahu G. Stroumsa, "Form(s) of God: Some Notes on Metatron and Christ," *Harvard Theological Review* 76 (1983): 269–88; Moshe Idel, *Kabbalah: New Perspectives* (New Haven, Conn., 1988), pp. 112–36; and Fishbane, "Some Forms of Divine Appearance in Jewish Thought."

22. Gershom Scholem, *Major Trends in Jewish Mysticism*, 3d rev. ed. (New York,

1961), p. 64, and pp. 63–67 in general. See Martin Samuel Cohen, *The Shi'ur Qomah: Liturgy and Theurgy in Pre-Kabbalistic Jewish Mysticism* (Lanham, Md., 1983), esp. pp. 99–109.

23. For the list of the powers and the animate limbs created in Adam, see chaps. 15–18 of the *Apocryphon*; for the creation of Adam's material body, see 21:1–13. An English translation of the text, "The Secret Book According to John," can be found in *The Gnostic Scriptures*, trans. Bentley Layton (Garden City, N.Y., 1987), pp. 39–45.

24. For a comparable treatment of the rhetorical and cultural construction of the imperial cult, see S. R. F. Price, *Rituals and Power: The Roman Imperial Cult in Asia Minor* (Cambridge, 1984). See also Paul de Man, "Anthropomorphism and Trope in the Lyric," in *The Rhetoric of Romanticism* (New York, 1984), pp. 239–62. I also wish to acknowledge the influence upon my thinking of Yohanan Muffs's magisterial treatment of the personhood of God in the Bible in "Between Justice and Mercy: The Prayers of the Prophets" [Hebrew], in *Torah Nidreshet*, ed. A. Shapira (Tel Aviv, 1984), pp. 39–87, and of Alan Mintz's insightful discussion of the representation of God in Eikhah Rabbah in *Hurban* (New York, 1984), pp. 57–62.

25. The "essentialist" position is best represented in the critical tradition that goes from Henry James through E. M. Forster to Wayne Booth and much psychoanalytic criticism. By the nominalist tradition I mean mainly structuralist approaches to narrative from Propp through Greimas and Barthes. I wish to thank Alan Mintz for reminding me of this basic dichotomy in critical thinking about character.

26. The passage in its entirety, with both narratives, is found only in manuscripts of the Sephardic recension of Eikhah Rabbah. Most manuscripts of the Ashkenazic recension, including British Museum 27089, which Salomon Buber used for his edition of the petihtaot, lack both the second and the third interpretations of Isa. 22:12; see Buber, p. 25 nn. 15 and 16. In addition, two briefer versions of the passage are found in Midrash Eikhah Zuta, in *Midrash Zuta*, ed. Buber (Wilna, 1894), pp. 71–74 and 142–44 (found also in Yalkut Shimeoni, Eikha 4). Both of these versions have only the first narrative and part of the second, but not its beginning or end. I wish to express my gratitude to Paul Mandel for sharing with me his work on the recensions and the versions of this petihta.

Unfortunately, nothing is known about the background of these narratives. The only other Rabbinic narrative similar in style and language that I know of is the lengthy aggadah about the death of Moses in Tanhuma, Va'ethanan, in *Midrasch Tanhuma*, ed. Buber, 2 vols. (Wilna, 1885; reprint, Jerusalem, 1964), 2: Deuteronomy, 10–14, which uses some of the same unusual expressions and motifs.

27. For the Hebrew text, see Buber's edition of Eikhah Rabbah, pp. 25–28; for an English translation, see *Rabbinic Fantasies: Imaginative Narratives from Classical Hebrew Literature*, ed. David Stern and Mark Jay Mirsky (Philadelphia, 1990), pp. 47–57.

28. Hebrew: *shelo ezakeik lo*; for my translation, see Bereshit Rabbah 20:7, and Marcus Jastrow, *A Dictionary of the Targumim, the Talmud Babli and Yerushalmi, and the Midrashic Literature*, 2 vols. (1886–1903; reprint, New York, 1950), 1:410.

29. Note that it is only *after* the destruction that God is said actually to remove His presence, the Shekhinah, and return to heaven. The present text probably reflects a conflation of two motifs: first, the impossibility for the Temple to be destroyed as long as the divine presence protects it; second, the departure of the Shekhinah as a sign of the destruction that has occured. This somewhat uneasy conflation produces the nascent contradiction I have noted.

30. On the motif in the Bible, see Moshe Greenberg, *Ezekiel 1–20* (Garden City, N.Y., 1983), pp. 168–69, 200–202. On the ancient Near Eastern tradition, see in particular Piotr Michalowski, *The Lamentation over the Destruction of Sumer and Ur* (Winona Lake, Ind., 1989), pp. 45, 49, 53, 57–61, and the translation of the Tukulti-Ninurta epic in Peter Machinist, "Literature as Politics: The Tukulti-Ninurta Epic and the Bible," *Catholic Biblical Quarterly* 38 (1976): 455–82 (for discussion of the motif, pp. 462–64). Greenberg notes the relationship between these texts and the Ezekiel chapters (pp. 200–201), but no one, to my knowledge, has remarked upon their connection to the Rabbinic narratives or upon the striking parallels between the two portraits of God in the aggadah and the portraits of the separate deities Nanna-Su'en and Enlil in the ancient texts (see Greenberg's remarks on p. 201). In *In the Wake of the Goddesses: Women, Culture, and the Biblical Transformation of Pagan Myth* (New York, 1992), pp. 168–78, Tikvah Frymer-Kensky associates the motif of divine departure with the figure of Zion in the Bible.

31. See Norman J. Cohen, "Shekhinta Ba-Galuta: A Midrashic Response to Destruction and Persecution," *Journal for the Study of Judaism* 13 (1982): 147–59. See also the Yefei 'Anaf's comments, printed in the folio edition of Midrash Rabbah, pp. 6b–7a, suggesting that the character of God in the aggadah is actually a figure for the Community of Israel(!) and was never intended to represent God Himself, who, after all, could never possess the anthropopathic or anthropomorphic features ascribed to Him in the narrative!

32. On Metatron, see G. F. Moore, "Intermediaries in Jewish Thought," *Harvard Theological Review* 15 (1922): 62–85; Ephraim E. Urbach, *The Sages: Their Concepts and Beliefs*, trans. Israel Abrahams, 2 vols. (Jerusalem, 1975), 1:139; Stroumsa, "Form(s) of God," pp. 287–88.

33. See M. Berakhot 3:1.

34. The same indifferent voice is preserved in two fragmented versions of the episode about God's meeting with Abraham in the Temple: see B. Menahot 53b and Eikhah Rabbah ad Lam. 1:1 (Buber ed., p. 56). Both versions preserve the same playful exegesis of Jer. 11:16.

35. On the complaint as a genre, see my discussion in *Parables in Midrash*, pp. 130–45.

36. This case is argued by Galit Hasan-Rokem, who sees the figure of Rachel as a prototype of the feminine presence of God, in "My Sister's Voice: The Womanly Power of Lamentation, Mourning, and Love in Lamentations Rabbah," in *Women in Mediterranean Jewish Communities* [Hebrew], ed. Yael Atzmon (Jerusalem, 1995), 95–111. Compare Mintz's remarks in *Hurban,* p. 59, where he, too, attempts to distinguish the different characters of God along gender lines. Attractive as the interpretation may be, there is no evidence in this text (and hardly any support in any other Rabbinic text) that the Rabbinic God is ever anything but male. Professor Elliot Wolfson first called my attention to Moshe Idel's attempt in *Kabbalah,* pp. 128–36, to see a gender distinction and a sexualization of God in the phrase *du-partsufim;* but Idel's evidence is not fully convincing because his only real sources are either medieval-Kabbalistic or Philonic, not Rabbinic.

37. See Solomon Schechter, *Some Aspects of Rabbinic Theology* (New York, 1909), p. 37, who uses the phrase *imitatio hominis* to refer to God's performance of various mitzvot. Needless to say, this is a rather different meaning for the phrase than mine, but Schechter must be credited with inventing it (so far as I know). I wish to thank Professor Moshe Greenberg for calling this to my attention.

38. See, for example, the long aggadah about God learning how to mourn from the angels in Eikhah Rabbah 1:1 (Buber ed., pp. 42–43); and the two versions of the story of "the blood of Zechariah," in Eikhah Rabbah 3:13 (Buber ed., pp. 148–49) and petihta 23 (ibid., pp. 21–22), on which, see J. Heinemann, *Aggadot Vetoldoteihen* (Jerusalem, 1974), pp. 31–38.

39. On the two principles, see Urbach, *The Sages,* 1:448–61; Idel, *Kabbalah,* pp. 128–36.

40. Urbach, *The Sages,* 1:37–79; on the function of anthropomorphism, see p. 38.

41. According to Benjamin Zeev (Wilhelm) Bacher, *Aggadat Amorei Eretz Yisrael,* trans. A. Z. Rabinovitz (Tel Aviv, 1928), 1/1:32, this Hanina is Hanina ben Hama, a first-generation Amorah. Rabbi Berechiah, the author of the preceding opinion, was a fifth-generation Amorah. This line is therefore an editorial gloss; one should not mistakenly believe that the Rabbis were actually in disagreement the way the sequence of the text implies.

42. For another narrative of this sort, see Eikhah Rabbah 1:13 (Buber ed., pp. 75–76), translated and analyzed in Stern, *Parables in Midrash,* pp. 238–40.

43. Compare Mark Z. Brettler, *God Is King: Understanding an Israelite Metaphor* (Sheffield, 1989).

44. Fox, *Pagans and Christians*, pp. 93–94.

45. Paul Veyne, *Did the Greeks Believe in Their Myths?: An Essay on the Constitutive Imagination,* trans. Paula Wissing (Chicago, 1988).

46. Ibid., pp. 83–84.

47. Ibid., p. 23.

48. Ibid., p. 18. Compare Maimonides' remark, in *The Guide of the Perplexed*, trans. Shlomo Pines (Chicago, 1963), p. 102:

> The doctrine of the corporeality of God did not ever occur even for a single day to the Sages, may their memory be blessed, and that this was not according to them a matter lending itself to imagination or confusion. For this reason you will find that in the whole of the Talmud and in all the Midrashim they keep to the external sense of the dicta of the prophets. This is so because of their knowledge that this matter is safe from confusion and that with regard to it no error is to be feared in any respect; all the dicta have to be considered as parables and as a guidance conducting the mind toward one being.

49. By the term "destruction," I intend a partly mythical event including and transuming the historical destructions of both the first and second Temples. The Rabbis themselves had already begun to collapse the two events into a single memory. Thus it is difficult, perhaps intentionally so, to determine to which of the two destructions the narratives in Eikhah Rabbah refer. Except for one reference, in the last half of the second narrative, to the Jews exiled to Babylonia, there is no other historical specification in the text.

Index

Abahu, Rabbi, 64–65
Abba bar Kahana, Rabbi, 46, 48, 53
Abbaye, 17, 100 n 17
Akiba, Rabbi, 26, 65, 76–77, 92, 101 n. 26
The Alphabet of Rabbi Akiba, 18
Apocryphon of John, 78
Artemidorus, 100 n. 17
Auerbach, Erich, 51, 70
Augustine, Saint, 24–25, 70

Bana'ah, Rabbi, 100 n. 17
Bar Hedya, 100 n. 17
Bar Kappara, 39–40
Barthes, Roland, 8
Benjamin, Walter, 8
Berechiah, Rabbi, 44, 88–89
Bereshit Rabbah 1:1, 27–29, 104 n. 15; 1:15, 42–43; 8:3, 88–90; 22:19, 44; 27:1, 75
Blenkinsopp, Joseph, 30
Bloom, Harold, 8, 11–12, 32
Borges, Jorge Luis, 8
Boyarin, Daniel, 95 nn. 5–6

Derrida, Jacques, 15–16, 32, 98 n. 1

Eikhah Rabbah 3:21, 46–53; petihta 24, 80–86
Eleazar ben Azariah, Rabbi, 18–22, 33, 34–35, 38, 92, 101 n. 26
Eleazar Hisma, Rabbi, 35–37
Eliezer ben Hyrkanus, Rabbi, 30, 34

Freud, Sigmund, 11

Gamliel II, Rabban, 34–37
Goldin, Judah, 29

Die gottesdienstlichen Vortreage der Juden historisch entwickelt, 7

Hanina, Rabbi, 88–90
Hartman, Geoffrey, 1, 8, 12, 22
Hasan-Rokem, Galit, 114 n. 36
Heinemann, Isaac (Yitzhak), 7, 101 n. 24
Heinemann, Joseph, 7, 56–58
Hellerstein, Kathryn, 46
Herodotus, 91
Hoshaya, Rabbi, 27–28
House of Hillel, 21–22, 24, 42, 99 n. 10
House of Shammai, 21–22, 24, 42, 98 n. 10

Idel, Moshe, 114 n. 36
Iser, Wolfgang, 52
Ishmael, Rabbi, 76

Jabès, Edmond, 12
Jaffee, Martin, 95 n. 6
James, Henry, 50
Joshua ben Hananiah, Rabbi, 34–37
Joshua of Sikhnin, Rabbi, 65

Kabbalah and Criticism, 11
Kabbalah and Its Symbolism, 12
Kadushin, Max, 7
Kafka, Franz, 8, 11
Karaite sect, 26
Kermode, Frank, 25, 43

Lacan, Jacques, 16
Levi, Rabbi, 65
Lieberman, Saul, 45

Maimonides, 4, 43, 75, 115 n. 48
Marmorstein, Arthur, 76–77

Mekhilta de-Rabbi Ishmael, Bahodesh 4, 75; Shirta 3, 48
Midrash and Literature, 2
Mintz, Alan, 48, 114 n. 36
Mishnat Rabbi Eliezer, 18
Muffs, Yohanan, 112 n 24
Myers, David, 9

Neusner, Jacob, 77, 95–96 n. 6, 111 n. 18
New, Elisa, 96 n. 10

Pausanias, 92
Pesher Habakkuk, 23, 30–31
Pesikta de-Rav Kahana, 56; 1:223, 27
Philo, 24, 77
Pliny, 34

Raba, 100 n. 17
"Revelation and Tradition as Religious Categories in Judaism," 12
Ricoeur, Paul, 69
Roitman, Betty, 26

Saadiah Gaon, 75–76
The Sages, 87
Said, Edward, 37
Samuel ben Nahman, Rabbi, 80
Schechter, Solomon, 114 n. 37
Scholem, Gershom, 11, 12–13, 78
School of Rabbi Ishmael, 17–18
Sefer Hababir, 44
Shemot Rabbah 10:4, 92
Shimeon, Rabbi, 39–40
Shimeon ben Yohai, Rabbi, 44
Shi'ur Qomah, 78
Sifra, 48, 68
Sifre Deuteronomy 49, 29; 343, 48
Simon ben Gamliel, Rabban, 34
Steiner, George, 13
Steinschneider, Moritz, 9, 97 n. 16

Talmud, Babylonian: Baba Mezia 59b, 75; Eruvin 13b, 21; Hagigah 3a–b, 19, 35–37; Sanhedrin 34a, 17
Tanhum ben Rabbi Hanilai, Rabbi, 58–60
Tanna de-Bei Eliyahu, 43
The Turn of the Screw, 50

Ulpian, 46
Urbach, E. E., 69, 87

Vayikra Rabbah, 55–57, 68; 1:1, 58–63; 1:2–3, 64–66; 1:13–14, 63–64; 2:4, 44–45, 53; 28:2, 39–40
Veyne, Paul, 91–93

Wissenschaft des Judentums, 7, 9, 12
Wolfson, H. A., 77

Yermiyah, Rabbi, 30
Yerushalmi, Yosef Hayim, 10
Yohanan ben Beroka, Rabbi, 35–37
Yohanan ben Zakkai, Rabbi, 41
Yose Hagelili, Rabbi, 76
Yudan, Rabbi, 75

Zakhor, 10
Zhang Longxi, 15
Zohar, 44
Zunz, Leopold, 7, 10